About This Book

Why is this topic important?

Evaluation, training, and human performance technology (HPT) practitioners are faced with an increasing need to confirm the continuing efficiency, effectiveness, impact, and value of training programs and the continuing competence of learners. Yet within the literature related to instructional technology, educational technology, performance technology, and even evaluation itself, there is a lack of reference to *confirmative evaluation* as a distinct type of evaluation that goes beyond formative and summative evaluation to measure ongoing behavior, accomplishments (job outputs), and business results. This book is all about confirmative evaluation, an approach to evaluation that values the continuing merit, worth, and value of instruction over time.

What can you achieve with this book?

The purpose of the book is to ground the practice of confirmative evaluation in the literature on the theory and application of evaluation and research. The authors view evaluation as a technology in itself and suggest how to use hard and soft technology techniques and tools to plan and implement confirmative evaluation of training programs.

How is this book organized?

The book consists of nine chapters divided into three parts. Part One, "The Challenge," contains two chapters, which establish the conceptual framework for the book and present the systems-based procedural framework for confirmative evaluation: the Confirmative Evaluation Model. Part Two, "Meeting the Challenge," provides both theory and practice to help the reader master the art and science of confirmative evaluation. Each of the five chapters in this part focuses on one part of the process: preplanning, planning, doing, analyzing, and improving. Part Three, "Lessons from Oz," examines the "lions and tigers and bears" surrounding confirmative evaluation, presents a case study and looks at trends that are likely to have an impact on evaluation. The book concludes with a glossary of terms and a list of references.

About Pfeiffer

Pfeiffer serves the professional development and hands-on resource needs of training and human resource practitioners and gives them products to do their jobs better. We deliver proven ideas and solutions from experts in HR development and HR management, and we offer effective and customizable tools to improve workplace performance. From novice to seasoned professional, Pfeiffer is the source you can trust to make yourself and your organization more successful.

Essential Knowledge Pfeiffer produces insightful, practical, and comprehensive materials on topics that matter the most to training and HR professionals. Our Essential Knowledge resources translate the expertise of seasoned professionals into practical, how-to guidance on critical workplace issues and problems. These resources are supported by case studies, worksheets, and job aids and are frequently supplemented with CD-ROMs, websites, and other means of making the content easier to read, understand, and use.

Essential Tools Pfeiffer's Essential Tools resources save time and expense by offering proven, ready-to-use materials—including exercises, activities, games, instruments, and assessments—for use during a training or team-learning event. These resources are frequently offered in looseleaf or CD-ROM format to facilitate copying and customization of the material.

Pfeiffer also recognizes the remarkable power of new technologies in expanding the reach and effectiveness of training. While e-hype has often created whizbang solutions in search of a problem, we are dedicated to bringing convenience and enhancements to proven training solutions. All our e-tools comply with rigorous functionality standards. The most appropriate technology wrapped around essential content yields the perfect solution for today's on-the-go trainers and human resource professionals.

www.pfeiffer.com

Essential resources for training and HR professionals

ABOUT THE INSTRUCTIONAL TECHNOLOGY AND TRAINING SERIES

This comprehensive series responds to the rapidly changing training field by focusing on all forms of instructional and training technology—from the well-known to the emerging and state-of-the-art approaches. These books take a broad view of technology, which is viewed as systematized, practical knowledge that improves productivity. For many, such knowledge is typically equated with computer applications; however, we see it as also encompassing other nonmechanical strategies such as systematic design processes or new tactics for working with individuals and groups of learners.

The series is also based upon a recognition that the people working in the training community are a diverse group. They have a wide range of professional experience, expertise, and interests. Consequently, this series is dedicated to two distinct goals: helping those new to technology and training become familiar with basic principles and techniques, and helping those seasoned in the training field become familiar with cutting-edge practices. The books for both groups are rooted in solid research, but are still designed to help readers readily apply what they learn.

The Instructional Technology and Training Series is directed to persons working in many roles, including trainers and training managers, business leaders, instructional designers, instructional facilitators, and consultants. These books are also geared for practitioners who want to know how to apply technology to training and learning in practical, results-driven ways. Experts and leaders in the field who need to explore the more advanced, high-level practices that respond to the growing pressures and complexities of today's training environment will find indispensable tools and techniques in this groundbreaking series of books.

Rita C. Richey	Kent L. Gustafson
William J. Rothwell	M. David Merrill
Timothy W. Spannaus	Allison Rossett
Series Editors	*Advisory Board*

Confirmative Evaluation

Practical Strategies for Valuing Continuous Improvement

JOAN CONWAY DESSINGER

JAMES L. MOSELEY

Pfeiffer

A Wiley Imprint

www.pfeiffer.com

ISBN: 0-7879-6500-6

Library of Congress Cataloging-in-Publication Data

Dessinger, Joan Conway.
Confirmative evaluation: practical strategies for valuing continuous improvement / Joan Conway Dessinger and James L. Moseley.
    p. cm.
Includes index.
   ISBN 0-7879-6500-6 (alk. paper)
   1. Employees—Training of—Evaluation. I. Moseley, James L. (James Lee), 1942- II. Title.
   HF5549.5.T7D433 2004
   658.3'124—dc22

2003018776

Acquiring Editor: Matthew Davis
Director of Development: Kathleen Dolan Davies
Developmental Editor: Susan Rachmeler
Production Editor: Nina Kreiden

Editor: Thomas Finnegan
Manufacturing Supervisor: Bill Matherly
Editorial Assistant: Laura Reizman
Illustrations: Lotus Art

Printed in the United States of America

Printing   10 9 8 7 6 5 4 3 2 1

Thank you . . .

To all the evaluation, training, and HPT practitioners whose shared wisdom, experience, and humor fired the creation of this book

To family and friends who adapted to my schedule during the creation process

Joan Conway Dessinger

To my teachers, who inspire me . . .

To my students, who challenge me . . .

To my friends and fellow practitioners, who make evaluation work . . .

And to Midnite Moseley, for unconditional love, the fond and funny memories, and the once-in-a-lifetime friendship he shared . . .

My sincere thanks

James L. Moseley

CONTENTS

PART 1

The Challenge

PART 3

Lessons from Oz

LIST OF FIGURES, TABLES, AND PERFORMANCE SUPPORT TOOLS

Figures

Tables

Performance Support Tools (PSTs)

ACKNOWLEDGMENTS

THE AUTHORS WISH to acknowledge the following people:

Instructional Technology and Training series editors Rita Richey, William Rothwell, and Tim Spannaus

Pfeiffer editors Matt Davis, Kathleen Dolan Davies, Susan Rachmeler, Nina Kreiden, and Tom Finnegan

Joyce Wilkins, who assisted with production

David Solomon and April Davis, who supported and inspired us professionally

Kim Sneden and colleagues Paulla Wissel and Sara Weertz who walked us through Oz

Tore Stellas and Pete Jr., who introduced us to the concept "what you said would happen has happened"

HAVE YOU EVER . . .

Helped an employee maintain or continue to improve performance long after initial training or learning occurred?

Found that new contexts or new performance standards mandated a change in performance?

Experienced ineffective skill-building programs that had to be discarded, repurposed, or replaced?

Needed to determine how critical a particular performance factor was to organizational success?

Needed to establish that your training program has measurably improved business results?

If you answered yes to any of these questions, then read on . . .

This book is all about confirmative evaluation, "a new paradigm for continuous improvement" (Moseley and Solomon, 1997, p. 12). Confirmative evaluation verifies the continuing merit, worth, and value of instruction over time. Evaluation, training, and HPT (human performance technology) practitioners are faced with an increasing need to confirm the continuing efficiency, effectiveness, impact, and value of training programs and the continuing competence of learners. Yet within the literature related to instructional technology, educational technology, performance technology, and even evaluation itself, there is a lack of reference to confirmative evaluation as a distinct type of evaluation that goes beyond formative and summative evaluation to measure ongoing behavior, accomplishments (job outputs), and business results. Training practitioners themselves, when asked whether they have any experience with confirmative evaluation, tend to respond "Is that one of the four levels?" They are referring to Kirkpatrick's four levels of evaluation (Kirkpatrick, 1959, 1994).

Purpose

Confirmative Evaluation: Practical Strategies for Valuing Continuous Improvement sets out to fill the gap and provide a well-referenced and highly practical book for practitioners in training, evaluation, and HPT on why, when, and how to plan and conduct confirmative evaluation of training programs. The purpose of the book is to ground the practice of confirmative evaluation in the literature on the theory and application of evaluation and research. The *Instructional Technology and Training Series* focuses on instructional technology and training, so we view evaluation as a technology in itself and suggest how to use hard and soft technology techniques and tools to plan and implement confirmative evaluation of training programs.

Scope

This book presents an overview of full-scope evaluation (formative, summative, confirmative, and meta) using the Dessinger-Moseley Full-Scope Evaluation Model. The model also illustrates how confirmative evaluation fits within the current typology of evaluation. After a close-up look at full-scope evaluation, we present and discuss the Moseley-Dessinger Confirmative Evaluation

Model. The remainder of the book concentrates on how to use hard and soft technologies to plan and conduct an effective and efficient confirmative evaluation. We also suggest future directions for utilization of confirmative evaluation as an integral part of the technology of training and learning.

The focus of the *Instructional Technology and Training Series* is training. However, the theory and practice of confirmative evaluation applies to the evaluation of all performance improvement interventions, instructional and noninstructional. Therefore, we ask the reader to make a quantum leap whenever necessary to adapt the practical strategies in this book to noninstructional interventions such as incentive and reward programs, suggestion systems, career development initiatives, and so forth.

Audience

The audience for this series is a broad one. It goes beyond training to encompass all human performance improvement (HPI), evaluation, human resource development (HRD), management, and quality practitioners who are on the cutting edge of continuous improvement efforts. The audience also includes researchers and university professors or instructors in evaluation, instructional technology (IT), human performance technology (HPT), HRD, management, and related fields.

How This Book Is Organized

The book consists of nine chapters divided into three parts: "The Challenge," "Meeting the Challenge," and "Lessons from Oz." Each chapter is enhanced with figures, tables, and performance support tools. Real-world examples of confirmative evaluation are difficult to find; however, we use examples whenever possible to clarify concepts and offer on-the-job guidance for planning and conducting confirmative evaluation of training programs. We also include a glossary of terms and a list of references at the end of the book.

Part One: The Challenge

The first part contains two chapters. These opening chapters challenge the reader to take a risk and commit to full-scope evaluation. We encourage evaluators, training and HPT practitioners, and others to go beyond traditional formative and summative evaluation and add confirmative evaluation to their repertoire of knowledge and skills.

Chapter One: Full-Scope Evaluation: Raising the Bar

This chapter establishes the conceptual framework for the book and challenges evaluators and other professionals to raise the evaluation bar to include full-scope evaluation—formative, summative, confirmative, and meta.

Chapter Two: Confirmative Evaluation: A Model Guides the Way

The second chapter presents the systems-based procedural framework for confirmative evaluation, the Confirmative Evaluation Model. We walk the reader through the model using the inputs, processes, outputs, and outcomes of confirmative evaluation as a guide, and we also look into the heart of the model: meta evaluation. We end Part One with a discussion of the purpose and challenge of confirmative evaluation and how to justify using time, money, and human resources to plan and implement confirmative evaluation.

Part Two: Meeting the Challenge

The second part of this book lays out both theory and practice to help the reader master the art and science of confirmative evaluation. This part contains five chapters on the process components of the Confirmative Evaluation Model. Chapters Three and Four present *plan* as a two-step process: preplanning or evaluability assessment, and developing a confirmative evaluation plan. Chapters Five through Seven focus on the other process components of the Confirmative Evaluation Model: *do, analyze,* and *improve.* Chapters Three through Seven each contain a toolbox of additional references to help the evaluation, training, or HPT practitioner gain additional knowledge and skills related to the chapter topic.

Chapter Three: Preplan: Assess Training Program Evaluability

The first chapter in Part Two looks at the preplanning step in the confirmative evaluation planning process and stresses the importance of assessing the evaluability of the training program. We introduce a confirmative evaluation planning process flowchart and discuss the difference between proactive and reactive planning. Then we help the reader learn how to use the process flowchart plus a rating form and other performance support techniques and tools to assess the evaluability of a training program on the basis of criteria such as program life cycle, organization-specific requirements, stakeholder information needs, and intended evaluation outcomes.

Chapter Four: Plan: The Plan's the Thing

Chapter Four continues the discussion of the confirmative evaluation planning process by focusing on how to develop a confirmative evaluation plan and how to monitor the training program and maintain the plan if planning is proactive. We present two performance support tools: "Getting Started on a Confirmative Evaluation Plan" and a confirmative evaluation plan outline to help readers develop a complete, accurate, and useful confirmative evaluation plan. The chapter also discusses what happens after the plan is approved: reactive planners begin the confirmative evaluation, whereas proactive planners must maintain the plan for several months or more until it is time to conduct the confirmative evaluation. Planning a confirmative evaluation and preparing the confirmative evaluation plan require general project management skills, evaluation skills, analysis skills, and knowledge of how to evaluate learning and instruction technologies. So we give you a toolbox at the end of the chapter, a list of resources to help you increase your knowledge and skills in these areas.

Chapter Five: Do: For Goodness' Sake

Goodness is a term used by the military and others to indicate the degree to which people, places, situations, or things meet stated or implicit standards for excellence and integrity. In this chapter, we discuss how to use selected hard and soft technologies to conduct an efficient and effective confirmative evaluation. The topics include developing data-collection instruments, collecting the data, and documenting the process and the findings. Of course, there are challenges to face at every step, but we give you another toolbox of resources to meet those challenges.

Chapter Six: Analyze: Everything Old Is New Again

In Chapter Six, we focus again on hard and soft technologies, this time to analyze and interpret the data and communicate the results of the confirmative evaluation. This chapter contains practical suggestions and guidelines on how to analyze and interpret data and communicate the confirmative evaluation results. We differentiate between quantitative and qualitative data analysis, focus on analyzing and interpreting the confirmative evaluation results, spend some time outlining what constitutes an effective confirmative evaluation report, and present another toolbox—this time containing professional books and software packages to jump-start the analysis and communication process.

Chapter Seven: Improve: Now What?

This chapter presents the ultimate challenge: continuous quality improvement, assurance, and control. Once more the reader is encouraged to use the appropriate hard and soft technologies to support, implement, assure, and control the continuous quality improvement of the learners, the organization, and the global community. Resources in the toolbox at the end of the chapter include practical ways to apply the theory and practice of utilization-focused evaluation to confirmative evaluation and a self-assessment.

Part Three: Lessons from Oz

In the third part, we take a trip to Oz via a metropolitan zoo to examine the lions and tigers and bears surrounding confirmative evaluation; then we rub our crystal ball and acknowledge we're not in Oz anymore. Organizations, whether local or global, need full-scope evaluation to enable and support their continuous quality improvement efforts.

Chapter Eight: Case Study: Lions and Tigers and Bears, Oh My!

Pardon our whimsical side, but in this chapter we draw a parallel between Dorothy's journey to Oz and the development and evaluation of a training program or other instructional or noninstructional performance improvement interventions. There are even live lions and tigers and bears lurking in the shadows as we perform a meta evaluation of a confirmative evaluation of a training program for docents at a metropolitan zoo.

Chapter Nine: Conclusion: We're Not in Oz Anymore

The final chapter continues the journey to Oz as we look at trends and other challenges that affect program evaluation, continuous quality improvement, and technology. We also discuss evaluation as an emerging discipline, how to improve the confirmative evaluation process, and the qualities that make a stellar confirmative evaluator.

How to Use This Book

We foresee that evaluation, training, and HPI practitioners will use *Confirmative Evaluation: Practical Strategies for Valuing Continuous Improvement* as a desktop reference and that professors or instructors may use this book as a reference manual in the classroom. Even seasoned practitioners will find new insights and rules of thumb in its comprehensive presentations.

There are several approaches to using this book. Choose one or more of these suggestions to guide your understanding of and skill in using confirmative evaluation:

• Use this book as a just-in-time learning tool or as a performance support tool (PST). Skim the book to familiarize yourself with its layout. Each chapter builds on the preceding chapter or chapters. Look at the tables and figures. Review and use the PSTs. Refer to the Glossary for terminology with which you are unfamiliar. Know where you can find the information you need when you need it. Use the toolboxes at the end of Chapters Three through Seven to find additional, practical resources.

• Use the book as a primer. Learn about confirmative evaluation as a new evaluation paradigm, a process for ensuring and verifying the continuous improvement of instructional technology and training initiatives.

• View the book as a reference on the systemic approach to evaluation. It presents confirmative evaluation as a series of interrelated inputs, processes, outputs, and outcomes. Outputs of one event become the inputs of another event as the confirmative evaluation process moves toward the final outcome: continuous quality improvement of the learners, training program, work group, business, organization, or global community.

• Use this book to learn about full-scope evaluation and how to use proactive or reactive strategies for planning and conducting confirmative evaluation. Read the chapters as they are presented. Chapters One and Two set the tone and give an overview of full-scope evaluation and confirmative evaluation. Chapters Three through Seven are how-to guides for planning and conducting confirmative evaluation. Use the PSTs, and then discuss the outcomes with your team members for verification and validation. Explore the resources in the toolboxes for Chapters Three through Seven.

• Finally, just use this book for its value-added impact. The material in *Confirmative Evaluation* will benefit your organization (whether you represent business, industry, government, health care, or education) and you as an evaluation, training, or HPT practitioner.

October 2003   Joan Conway Dessinger, Ed.D., CPT
                                         The Lake Group
                                         St. Clair Shores, Michigan

                                         James L. Moseley, Ed.D., CPT
                                         Wayne State University
                                         Detroit, Michigan

Confirmative
Evaluation

PART 1

The Challenge

It's time to raise the bar on evaluation . . . and confirm that what we said would happen has happened.

1

Full-Scope Evaluation: Raising the Bar

SEELS AND RICHEY (1994, p. 52) call evaluation "a commonplace human activity" and indicate that as far back as the 1930s instructional designers, evaluators, and other training/HPT (human performance technology) practitioners discussed, wrote about, and sometimes implemented evaluation activities to measure the value of training and learning. The evaluation bar was raised in 1967 when Scriven suggested that exemplary instructional designers and evaluators plan and conduct two types of evaluation: *formative evaluation,* to improve instructional programs or products during the development phase; and *summative evaluation,* to measure the effectiveness of education, training, and learning during or immediately after implementation. The terms *formative* and *summative* have "not only served the field well in providing a usable language to describe important uses of evaluation, but have also been a rich conceptual seedbed for the sprouting of many proposed refinements and extensions to the field" (Worthen, Sanders, and Fitzpatrick, 1997, p. 18). Now it's time to raise the bar again.

We challenge evaluation, training, and HPT practitioners to add confirmative evaluation to their repertoire of knowledge and skills. Confirmative evaluation goes beyond formative and summative evaluation to judge the continuing merit, value, or worth of a long-term training program. More specifically, we challenge training and evaluation practitioners to consistently use full-scope evaluation: formative, summative, confirmative, and meta. Confirmative evaluation encourages and supports continuous improvement efforts within organizations. Meta evaluation evaluates evaluation and adds credibility to evaluation activities. However, meta evaluation is another story and another book. Meanwhile, we need to focus on confirmative evaluation.

In this chapter, we set the stage for confirmative evaluation. First, we introduce the concept of full-scope evaluation as an integrated plan that uses four types of evaluation—formative, summative, confirmative, and meta— to judge the continuing merit and worth of long-term training programs. We use models to illustrate how the four types of evaluation work together and how full-scope evaluation fits into the instructional system design (ISD) process. Then we discuss the challenges faced by individuals and organizations that commit to full-scope evaluation.

One issue that arose when we began writing this book is that although there is common evaluation vocabulary, there is limited shared meaning. When discussing evaluation, the literature uses the words *types, roles, stages, phases,* and *forms* of evaluation. For consistency, we use the word *type* when referring to formative, summative, and confirmative evaluation.

After reading this chapter, you will be able to:

1. Explain the concept of full-scope evaluation

2. Describe and compare the components of full-scope evaluation (formative, summative, confirmative, and meta evaluation)

3. Explain how full-scope evaluation turns ADDIE into ADDI/E (more on this later; also, see the Glossary at the end of the book)

4. Recognize the challenges associated with committing to full-scope evaluation

Evaluation: The Full Scope

Full-scope evaluation systematically judges the merit and worth of a long-term training program before, during, and after implementation. Full-scope evaluation is appropriate only for training programs that are designed to run for one year or more; it is not appropriate for a one-time training event, such as a single-session workshop to introduce a new product to sales representatives.

Full-scope evaluation integrates four types of program evaluation—formative, summative, confirmative, and meta—into the training program evaluation plan (see Chapter Three). Working together, the four types of evaluation help to determine the value of a long-term training program and develop the business case or rationale for maintaining, changing, discarding, or replacing the program. We describe all four types of evaluation here.

Formative Evaluation

Formative evaluation is the oldest type of evaluation. Scriven (1967) was the first to use the term; however, the concept and practice of evaluating instruction during development predated both the term and the ISD movement (Tessmer, 1994). Thiagarajan (1991) defines and describes formative evaluation from a quality perspective as "a quality control method to improve, not prove, instructional effectiveness" (p. 22) and "a continuous process incorporated into different stages of development" (p. 26). Dick and King (1994) add that formative evaluation is a way to ". . . facilitate the transfer of learning from the classroom to the performance context" (p. 8).

Formative evaluation is usually conducted by the designer or developer; however, large organizations sometimes call on the services of a practitioner evaluator. Van Tiem, Moseley, and Dessinger (2000) describe four basic strategies for conducting formative evaluation:

1. Expert review using an individual or group familiar with the content and need

2. One-to-one evaluation involving the designer or evaluator and a learner or performer

3. Live or virtual small-group evaluation

4. Field testing or piloting either segments or all of the program or product (pp. 164–167)

The outputs and outcomes of formative evaluation mold the training program and set the stage for summative evaluation of immediate program results. Therefore the primary customers of formative evaluation are the instructional designers and developers who are responsible for selecting or developing the instructional performance support system or training package.

Summative Evaluation

Summative evaluation "involves gathering information on adequacy and using this information to make decisions about utilization" (Seels and Richey, 1994, p. 57). Summative evaluation is conducted during or immediately after implementation. There is also a purposeful difference between formative and summative evaluation: "If the purpose of evaluation is to improve . . . then it is formative evaluation. (In contrast, if the purpose is to prove, justify, certify, make a 'go/no' decision, or validate . . . then it is summative evaluation.)" (Thiagarajan, 1991, p. 22).

The primary customers are the decision makers who need to approve installation of the instructional performance support system, or in the case of a one-time offering put a final seal of approval on the instructional package. These decision makers may or may not participate in earlier instructional design and development activities. In either case, they need immediate feedback from the first session or the first several sessions: How well did the training meet the stated instructional objectives? How well did it meet expectations of the instructor(s) and participants?

During summative evaluation, "any aspect of the total education or training system can be evaluated: the student, the instructor, instructional strategies, the facilities, even the training organization itself" (Smith and Brandenburg, 1991, p. 35). The designer/developer or evaluator may select from or blend a number of strategies for conducting summative evaluation: cost-benefit analysis, attitude ratings (student, instructor, client, and other stakeholders), testing (pre-, post-, embedded, and performance tests), surveys, observation, interviews, focus groups, and statistical analysis. The focus is on immediate results; in a situation involving a long-term program, the outputs and outcomes of summative evaluation become inputs for the next step, confirmative evaluation.

Confirmative Evaluation

Confirmative evaluation goes beyond formative and summative evaluation; it moves traditional evaluation a step closer to full-scope evaluation. During confirmative evaluation, the evaluation, training, or HPT practitioner collects, analyzes, and interprets data related to behavior, accomplishment, and results in order to determine "the continuing competence of learners or the continuing effectiveness of instructional materials" (Hellebrandt and Russell, 1993, p. 22) and to verify the continuous quality improvement of education and training programs (Mark and Pines, 1995).

The concept of going beyond formative and summative evaluation is not new. The first reference to confirmative evaluation came in the late 1970s: "The formative-summative description set ought to be expanded to include a third element, *confirmative evaluation*" (Misanchuk, 1978, p. 16). Eight years later, Beer and Bloomer (1986) from Xerox suggested a limited strategy for going beyond the formative and summative distinctions in evaluation by focusing on three levels for each type of evaluation:

1. Level one: evaluate programs while they are still in draft form, focusing on the needs of the learners and the developers

2. Level two: continue to monitor programs after they are fully implemented, focusing on the needs of the learners and the program objectives

3. Level three: assess the transfer of learning to the real world

Geis and Smith (1992, p. 133) report: "The current emphasis is on evaluation as a means of finding out what is working well, why it is working well, and what can be done to improve things." However, when the quality movement gained prominence and business thinking raised the bar, educators and trainers began to agree, at least in principle, that "quality control requires continuous evaluation including extending the cycle beyond summative evaluation" (Seels and Richey, 1994, p. 59). Summative evaluation has immediate usefulness, but it does not help planners make decisions for the future. Confirmative evaluation, on the other hand, is future-oriented; it focuses on enduring, long-term effects or results over the life cycle of an instructional or noninstructional performance intervention: "Enduring or long-term effects refer to those changes that can be identified after the passage of time and are directly linked to participation in [education or training]" (Hanson and Siegel, 1995, pp. 27–28).

A Rose by Any Other Name

Since Misanchuk (1978) coined the term, there has been a marked lack of reference to confirmative evaluation. Even so, within the literature related to the design of research there are references to *stability over time, repeated measures, retention studies, recidivism* (tendency to return to a former pattern), and *time series* (S. B. Sawilowsky, personal communication, June 5, 2001). "In education and psychology, terms such as *follow-up studies, longitudinal studies,* and *ex-post-facto studies* have reflected the existence of related concepts, as well as the need for such additional evaluations" (Hellebrandt and Russell, 1993, p. 22). In their book on using an ISD model to enhance the role of training in large organizations, Hannum and Hansen (1989) describe two types of evaluation, summative and follow-up: "The second type of evaluation occurs some time after the instruction and is called follow-up evaluation. Its purpose is to evaluate how and if the training is being used by the participants and is used to determine the overall success of the training program. . . . Follow-up data may be collected some months as well as years after participants attend a given training session. . . . Once the data are gathered, they are then analyzed over time to determine overall success and the program is revised as needed" (pp. 36–37).

Rae (1999) uses the term *post-program* evaluation and describes three levels of follow-up evaluation: "Too often evaluation (or what passes for it) does not extend beyond the end of programme validation, but then all that has been assessed is the satisfaction of the training programme objectives and the immediate objectives of the learners. This goes some way if it has been performed effectively, but it is not complete evaluation and certainly does not lead to an assessment of the value effectiveness of the learning. In order to do this, three further stages are necessary: Post-programme debriefing, medium term evaluation, [and] longer term evaluation" (p. 167).

The quality literature also contains references that imply confirmative evaluation. In addition to the term *continuous improvement,* there are also references to *quality control* and *quality assurance*: "The terms gaining greater acceptance in business training are *quality control* for input and process functions and *quality assurance* for product or output functions" (Brandenburg, 1989, pp. 85–86). As Seels and Richey (1994) state, "The quality improvement movement will affect the evaluation domain. Quality control requires continuous evaluation including extending the cycle beyond summative evaluation" (p. 59).

Two other terms related to confirmative evaluation are *outcome evaluation* and *impact evaluation.* According to Schalock (1995), outcome-based evaluation is "a type of program evaluation that used valued and objective person-referenced outcomes to analyze a program's effectiveness, impact, or cost-benefit" (p. 5). Further, impact evaluation looks at negative or positive program based changes in performance and focuses on "whether the program made a difference compared to either no program or an alternate program" (p. 6). Although outcome and impact evaluation are not synonymous with confirmative evaluation, confirmative evaluation does contain elements of both outcome and impact evaluation.

Even level four of Kirkpatrick's four levels of evaluation (1959, 1994) is confirmative evaluation by another name. Level four measures the results of training in terms of change in participant behavior and "tangible results that more than pay for the cost of training" (1994, p. 69).

Meta Evaluation

Formative, summative, and confirmative evaluation are all fodder for meta evaluation. Meta evaluation ". . . is a quality control process that is applied to the processes, products and results of formative, summative, and confirmative evaluation" (Van Tiem, Moseley, and Dessinger, 2000, p. 181). It is all about evaluating the evaluation. The evaluator literally zooms in on how the evaluation was conducted. The purpose of meta evaluation is to validate the evaluation inputs, process, outputs, and outcomes. It serves as a learning process for the evaluator and makes the evaluators accountable: "Evaluators will be more likely to see their studies effectively utilized when they demonstrate that their work can stand the test of careful analysis and that they themselves are open to growth through constructive criticism" (Posavac and Carey, 1989, pp. 281–282).

There are two types of meta evaluation: type one and type two. Table 1.1 describes the two types of meta evaluation in terms of timing and purpose.

Table 1.1. Meta Evaluation: Type, Timing, and Purpose.

Type	Timing	Purpose
Type one (formative)	Conducted during formative, summative, and confirmative evaluation	Guides the evaluator through the planning, design, and implementation of all three stages of evaluation
Type two (summative)	Conducted after the formative, summative, and confirmative evaluations are completed	Provides feedback on the reliability and validity of the evaluation processes, products, and results

Source: Van Tiem, D. M., Moseley, J. L., and Dessinger, J. C. *Fundamentals of Performance Technology: A Guide to Improving People, Process, and Performance.* © 2000 International Society for Performance Improvement. p. 181. Reprinted with permission.

Type one meta evaluation is conducted concurrently with the evaluation process. It is literally a formative evaluation of evaluation. Type two meta evaluation is the more common approach. It is conducted after formative, summative, and at least one cycle of confirmative evaluation is completed. Stufflebeam (1978) and The Joint Committee on Standards for Educational Evaluation (1994) offer an extensive set of utility, feasibility, propriety, and accuracy standards and guidelines for conducting a type two meta evaluation in education or training settings.

Comparing the Four Types of Evaluation

Table 1.2 illustrates a comparison of the four types of evaluation. The constructs used for comparison are timing, purpose, and customers.

Table 1.2. Evaluation Types: Timing, Purpose, and Customers.

Type	Timing	Purpose	Customers
Formative	During design, development, and pilot or field testing	Improve analysis, design, development processes, and outputs	**Primary:** design team (designers, developers, instructors, subject matter experts, etc.) **Secondary:** decision makers and customers
Summative	During or immediately after full implementation	Assess immediate results (outputs and outcomes)	**Primary:** decision makers and customers **Secondary:** design team (designers, developers, instructors, subject matter experts, etc.)
Confirmative	3–12 months after full implementation	Assess effectiveness, efficiency, impact, and value over time	**Primary:** decision makers and users **Secondary:** design team (designers, developers, instructors, subject matter experts, etc.)
Meta	**Type one:** concurrent with development and implementation **Type two:** after development and implementation	Validate evaluation process, products, outputs	**Primary:** evaluators **Secondary:** decision makers and users

Source: Dessinger (2002).

Timing

Like summative evaluation, confirmative evaluation takes place after development and implementation. Hellebrandt and Russell (1993) state that confirmative evaluation should occur six months to one year after development and initial implementation, depending on the criticality, complexity, and frequency of the learning or performance. Carr (1992, p. 151) is even more aggressive, suggesting that confirmative evaluation of ongoing training programs "should begin the day the first training ends."

If we consider confirmative evaluation in terms of *assessing impact,* Rossi, Freeman, and Lipsey (1999) insist that "interventions should be evaluated for impact only when they have been in place long enough to have ironed out implementation problems" (p. 238). Implementation problems may include failure to deliver critical elements to appropriate targets, lack of measurable outcomes, or lack of summative or formative evaluation data. For example, during the implementation of a recent leadership training program, individual instructors selected modules that they felt best suited the audience for a particular session; they did not present the entire program. Some instructors also decided not to conduct summative evaluation at the end of their sessions because the sessions ran over the allotted time and the participants were eager to leave.

Performance Support Tool (PST) 1.1 is a decision matrix that helps the practitioner decide when to implement a confirmative evaluation on the basis of the criticality, complexity, and frequency of the training program's intended learning or performance outcomes.

PST 1.1. When to Conduct a Confirmative Evaluation.

Purpose: To help you decide when to conduct a confirmative evaluation on the basis of the criticality, complexity, and frequency of the learning or performance.

Directions: Ask all the stakeholders to rate the training program according to the criteria in the first column. Then decide when to confirm the outcomes of the training program.

Learning/Performance Factor	Rating	Confirm Every . . .
Criticality: How critical is the learning/performance to the success of the organization?	☐ High ☐ Medium ☐ Low	☐ 3–6 months ☐ 6–12 months ☐ 12 months
Complexity: How complex is the learning/performance?	☐ High ☐ Medium ☐ Low	☐ 3–6 months ☐ 6–12 months ☐ 12 months
Frequency: How often is the learning/performance required?	☐ Regularly ☐ Monthly ☐ Annually ☐ One time only	☐ 6–12 months ☐ 6–12 months ☐ 12 months ☐ Do not confirm
Frequency: How often is the learning/performance implemented?	☐ Regularly ☐ Monthly ☐ Annually ☐ One time only	☐ 6–12 months ☐ 6–12 months ☐ 12 months ☐ Do not confirm

Source: Van Tiem, D. M., Moseley, J. L., and Dessinger, J. C. *Fundamentals of Performance Technology: A Guide to Improving People, Process, and Performance.* Copyright © 2000 International Society for Performance Improvement. p. 180. Used with permission.

Suggested start-up targets range from three months to one year after the implementation of the training program. If the learning or performance outcomes of the training program are highly critical to the success of the organization or are very complex, the program should undergo confirmative evaluation between three and six months after implementation. On the other hand, an evaluator may wait a year to conduct confirmative evaluation of a training program whose learning or performance outcomes are rated low in criticality or complexity. There is no need to conduct a confirmative evaluation if the learning or performance outcomes take place only one time or infrequently—for example, a training program on how to develop an organization's five-year strategic plan.

Purpose

Formative and summative evaluation each zoom in on needs, processes, products, reactions, and accomplishments. The purpose of formative evaluation is to validate the needs analysis and the training program design process and outputs; the purpose of summative evaluation is to assess the participant's accomplishments during and immediately after training. Confirmative evaluation zooms out to take a long-term view of the effectiveness, efficiency, impact, and value of a training program. The purpose of confirmative evaluation is twofold: (1) identify, explain, and confirm or justify the continuing value of training and learning over time; and (2) help decision makers manage the instructional performance support system and the learner over time (Van Tiem, Moseley, and Dessinger, 2000).

Customers

The primary customers for formative evaluation are the program designers and developers; the primary customers for summative and confirmative evaluation could include any or all of the internal and external stakeholders, that is, anyone who has a vested interest (expressed as need or expectation) in the process, outputs, and outcomes of the training program. Shrock and Geis (1999) support the concept that the customer base for summative evaluation may be broader because traditionally "much of the feedback used to make revisions to an intervention is collected after an intervention is implemented" (p. 192).

The primary customers of confirmative evaluation are long-term decision makers. Executives, managers, consultants, and others may use the outputs and outcomes of confirmative evaluation for strategic planning. Other decision makers use the results of confirmative evaluation to determine whether to maintain, improve, discard, or replace the training program or noninstructional performance intervention. In addition, decision makers involved with certification processes have a special stake in confirmative evaluation outcomes. For example, "The notion of confirmative evaluation is significant in the health professions in terms of assuring that learners maintain their clinical knowledge and skills. . . . Confirmative evaluation in nursing is significant, particularly in the clinical setting, to assure that learners maintain their competencies and to identify where additional review and practice are needed" (Oermann and Gaberson, 1998, p. 5).

Evaluation: Full-Scope Model

Going beyond formative and summative evaluation ". . . challenges us to jettison linear models and integrate evaluative processes throughout every phase of ISD" (Moseley and Solomon, 1997, p. 12), not just add evaluation at the end, as implied by the traditional ADDIE (analyze, design, develop, implement, evaluate) model. The Dessinger-Moseley 360° Evaluation Model (Moseley and Dessinger, 1998) illustrates the integration of evaluation throughout the ISD process (ADDI/E) and presents six foci for integrating evaluation activities: need, design and development, reaction, accomplishment, transfer, and impact. The model was influenced by the work of Seels and Richey (1994); Kirkpatrick (1994); Kaufman, Keller, and Watkins (1996); and Brinkerhoff (1987).

Figure 1.1, the Dessinger-Moseley Full-Scope Evaluation Model, expands the earlier 360° model by adding *value* to the foci and by introducing the concept of full-scope evaluation.

Figure 1.1. Dessinger-Moseley Full-Scope Evaluation Model.

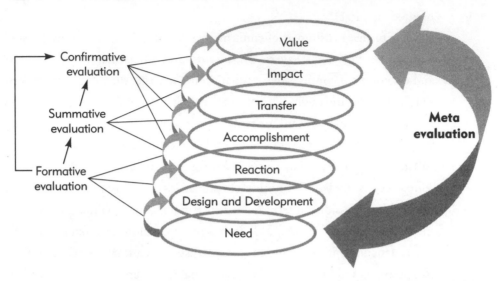

The spiraling concentric circles of the Full-Scope Evaluation Model represent the "proactive and iterative nature of evaluation" (Moseley and Dessinger, 1998, p. 247). Within the circles are the focal points for each type of evaluation:

- Need for training

- Instructional design and development processes and products

- Reaction during and after training

- Accomplishment during training

- On-the-job transfer of new knowledge, skills, or attitudes

- Impact of negative or positive training results on the individual, business group, organization, or global community

- Value to the individual, business group, organization, and global community

The center of the model illustrates the foci for formative, summative, and confirmative evaluation:

- Formative evaluation focuses on need, design and development, and pre-implementation reaction and accomplishment
- Summative evaluation focuses on the immediate results of program implementation: reaction; accomplishment; and the self-reported expectation that new knowledge, skills, and attitudes will transfer to the job and affect workplace performance
- Confirmative evaluation focuses on the program's continuing impact and value, as well as long-term transfer, accomplishment, and reaction

The left side of the model emphasizes that input from formative evaluation flows into summative and confirmative evaluation; input from summative evaluation flows into confirmative evaluation, and each type of evaluation has its own set of evaluation foci. On the right side of the model, the process of meta evaluation focuses on all the evaluation types—their inputs, outputs, outcomes, and foci.

Challenges to Full-Scope Evaluation

Full-scope evaluation is not without challenges. Daring to go beyond the traditional formative and summative framework is the first challenge. Added to this are demands created by the new organization of the twenty-first century, context factors specific to an organization, and the challenge of overcoming the "success syndrome." All these challenges are interrelated and call for strong action from the evaluation, training, or HPT practitioner.

Daring to Go Beyond Formative and Summative Evaluation

Full-scope evaluation should be the norm rather than the exception. More and more, training is considered an integral part of strategic planning. As investments in training increase, there is a corresponding increase in the "expectation that workplace improvement practitioners rigorously measure the outcomes that these investments produce, and in so doing, generate the insight and understanding necessary to continuously improve those outcomes" (Bassi and Ahlstrand, 2000, p. 1). However, even more enlightened organizations still view evaluation as a costly add-on rather than a value-added activity. They think of full-scope evaluation in terms of how much the additional time, money, and other resources will cost. The practitioner may even find that "either there is no positive consequence for human resources or training in demonstrating business results, or there are actually disincentives" (Binder, 2002a, p. 8). It's hard to dare to think outside the box when the organization does not support, or even punishes, such thinking.

Adapting to the New Organization

Despite current lack of support for full-scope evaluation, futurists see a new organization emerging in the twenty-first century. Reed (2002, pp. 24–25) suggests that this new organization requires a new way of looking at training: "Training's definition should be the provision of learning opportunities for successful performance improvement . . . training must also be seen as a process that is continuous and learner centric; one that focuses on the pull or output side." The focus on results challenges organizations and training departments to take a new look at evaluation in general and confirmative evaluation in particular. The practitioner needs new knowledge and skill to function as a change agent and a cheerleader for full-scope evaluation.

Adjusting for Context Factors

Context factors also create a challenge. Context factors include organizational culture, climate, and environment and are often codified in the organization's mission, values, and goals. To implement full-scope evaluation, the total organization must:

- Recognize the long-term value of education, training, and learning
- Actively support the concepts of accountability and continuous improvement

- Recognize the value of full-scope evaluation of education, training, and learning
- Commit to full-scope evaluation
- Actively support full-scope evaluation

In turn, the evaluation, training, or HPT practitioner, and stakeholders who are involved in the planning and implementing of full-scope evaluation must:

- Know the mission, goals, and values of the organization
- Agree with the mission, goals, and values of the organization
- Value and buy into the mission, goals, and values of the organization
- Support the organization by aligning evaluation outcomes with the mission, goals, values, and culture of the organization

"Know your organization" is the caveat and challenge that can guide internal and external evaluation, training, and HPT practitioners to the successful implementation of full-scope evaluation.

Overcoming the "Success Syndrome"

One final challenge is the success syndrome: the tendency for individuals and organizations to use positive outputs from summative evaluation to trigger a decision not to proceed with full-scope evaluation. Consistently high positive participant reaction forms or consistently low pretest and high posttest scores are the major culprits.

In one example, decision makers from a division of a major automotive company approved a full-scope evaluation plan for a new, long-term, basic-skills training program. However, the early summative evaluation results at level one (did they like it?) and level two (did they learn?) were so positive that the decision makers decided to save money by discontinuing *all* types and levels of evaluation. The training program continued unchanged for three more years, and then the participant materials were distributed over the company intranet as part of new-employee orientation. Finally, the online program was absorbed into a corporate university curriculum, where it died a natural death—no one signed up for the course.

SUMMARY: LESSONS LEARNED IN CHAPTER ONE

1. Full-scope evaluation includes formative, summative, confirmative, and meta evaluation.

2. Confirmative evaluation is a new paradigm for continuous improvement.

3. Full-scope evaluation turns ADDIE process into ADDI/E because it integrates evaluation throughout the ISD process.

4. Challenges to full-scope evaluation include daring to go beyond formative and summative evaluation, adapting to the new organization of the 21st century, adapting to context factors, and overcoming the success syndrome.

5. Personal lessons learned:

_____

_____

_____

_____

_____

_____

_____

_____

_____

NEXT STEPS

Chapter Two introduces the Moseley-Dessinger Confirmative Evaluation Model and discusses the model components, justifies using confirmative evaluation, and presents challenges to successful confirmative evaluation.

2

Confirmative Evaluation: A Model Guides the Way

NOW THAT WE HAVE INTRODUCED you to the concept and challenges of full-scope evaluation, it's time to get close up and personal with the least-known and least-practiced type of evaluation in the full-scope evaluation repertoire, confirmative evaluation. We have developed the Confirmative Evaluation Model in this chapter to illustrate the process of confirmative evaluation using inputs, process, outputs, and outcomes. In this chapter, we also explain why meta evaluation is at the center of the Confirmative Evaluation Model, present some specific challenges faced by those who plan and implement confirmative evaluation, and end the chapter by suggesting some answers to the inevitable question, "Why bother?"

After reading this chapter, you will be able to:

1. Explain the Confirmative Evaluation Model in terms of input, process, output, and outcome and the role of meta evaluation

2. Explain how soft technology inputs have an impact on successful confirmative evaluation

3. Discuss the link between continuous improvement and confirmative evaluation

4. Recognize the challenges specific to planning and conducting confirmative evaluation

5. Discuss each challenge and its applicability to evaluation practice

6. Identify additional challenges that are specific to your organization's culture or the skills of the current evaluation personnel

7. Answer the question, "Why bother?"

Confirmative Evaluation Model

"The process of evaluation, like any other process, can be studied in terms of the inputs, outputs, and processes" (Thiagarajan, 1991, p. 22). In the Confirmative Evaluation Model (Figure 2.1), we visually represent confirmative evaluation as a systematic, iterative process with inputs, processes, outputs, and outcomes. The model does not prescribe a linear approach but instead encourages the evaluator or evaluation team to move back and forth between the components of the model as needed, adding new input, producing new outputs, and delivering continuous improvement outcomes.

Inputs to Confirmative Evaluation

Inputs is a collective term. It refers to anything that a system or a system component receives from its larger universe, including requirements, restraints, and resources. In the case of an event- or activity-based system such as confirmative evaluation, inputs may include information, people, energies, materials, and other resources (Banathy, 1991). Inputs may occur at various times during confirmative evaluation planning and implementation and may be classified as direct or indirect.

Direct Inputs to Confirmative Evaluation. Outputs from formative, summative, and type one meta evaluation produce direct inputs to confirmative evaluation. The outputs of formative evaluation may include problem identification, cause analysis, recommendations for improvement, and appropriate

Figure 2.1. Moseley-Dessinger Confirmative Evaluation Model.

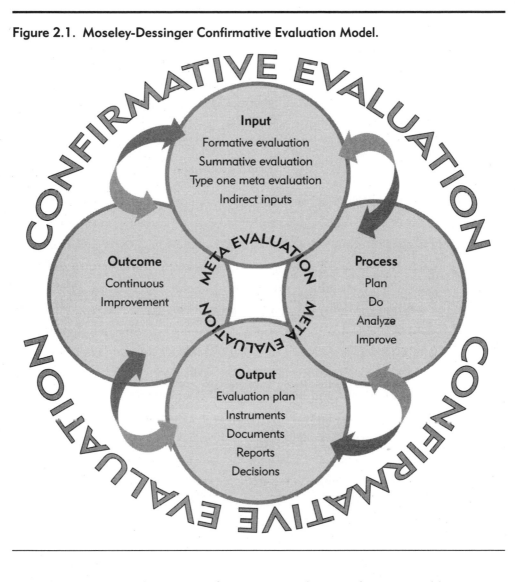

revisions. The outputs of summative evaluation of training and learning are the answers to two questions: How good is it? Does it meet our needs? (Smith and Brandenburg, 1991, p. 35).

The outputs of summative evaluation may include findings and recommendations related to learner reaction, instructional effectiveness, and the immediate acquisition and transfer of learning. The outcome of summative evaluation is the establishment of the immediate value of training as "an objective basis for decision-making" (Van Tiem, Moseley, and Dessinger, 2000, p. 171).

Type one and type two meta evaluation are both useful for validating the inputs, processes, outputs, and outcomes of confirmative evaluation. For example, type one meta evaluation validates formative and summative evaluation processes, outputs, and outcomes in real-time and therefore validates the inputs to confirmative evaluation; type two provides after-the-fact evaluation of formative, summative, and confirmative evaluation.

Indirect Inputs to Confirmative Evaluation. Commitment to full-scope evaluation and soft technologies such as instructional, performance, communication, and change technology produces indirect inputs to confirmative evaluation. Commitment ensures that confirmative evaluation will happen; soft technology inputs are primarily techniques and tools that help guide the process.

Although confirmative evaluation is heavily reliant on the outputs and outcomes of formative and summative evaluation, these outputs and outcomes are only as good as the level of stakeholder commitment to full-scope evaluation. Commitment to full-scope evaluation is therefore an essential if indirect input to confirmative evaluation. Confirmative evaluation does not happen unless the stakeholders also commit to going beyond formative and summative evaluation and implementing full-scope evaluation. Without confirmative evaluation, the practitioner cannot respond to a client's need to know whether a long-term training program was successful in terms of tangible and intangible benefits to the organization.

Technology is all about systematically applying knowledge to improve performance. The major difference between soft and hard technologies is the reliance on a man-machine interface. Instructional technology (IT) and human performance technology are commonly referred to as *soft* technologies because they systematically apply the knowledge and experience of people with or without the use of hard technology such as computers and telecommunication technology. Soft technologies generate important indirect inputs to the confirmative evaluation process:

• Instructional and HPT practitioners use evaluation to prove and improve the results and value of training and other performance interventions. The conceptual and practice-based literature from these two fields, along with the literature from the field of research and evaluation, is building a solid, theoretical foundation for all evaluation practices, even when those practices go beyond formative and summative.

• Communication technology, which systematically applies the knowledge gained from research into auditory, visual, and kinesthetic thinking, learning, and message transmission, is critical to the successful planning and implementation of the communication elements in the confirmative evaluation process. For example, research on psychological, cultural, political, graphical, and other communication elements can influence the effectiveness of support-gathering activities, data-collection techniques and instruments, information dissemination, and reporting.

• Change technology also creates a strong foundation for confirmative evaluation activities. Research and practice in how to plan, implement, and evaluate change in individuals and organizations should drive the entire confirmative evaluation process toward a successful final outcome: continuous quality improvement.

Process of Confirmative Evaluation

Process is action that occurs over a period of time and turns inputs into outputs. The process may "either (1) make adjustments and correct for differences between the actual and desired output, or (2) change the system itself" (Banathy, 1991, p. 102).

Certain activities are conducted during all types of evaluation: "Evaluation activities generally fall into five phases—planning, materials development, data collection, analysis, and reporting" (Smith and Brandenburg, 1991, p. 36). The process for confirming the continuing value of a training program is no exception.

Moseley and Solomon (1997) used Walter Shewhart's continuous improvement cycle (plan, do, check, act) as the basis for labeling the elements of the confirmative evaluation process. Our Confirmative Evaluation Model reaffirms the link to continuous quality improvement by referring to the confirmative evaluation process as *plan, do, analyze, improve*:

- *Plan* is all about identifying and understanding the "W^{5}H"—the who, what, where, when, why, and how—of a confirmative evaluation. The output is a blueprint for conducting a confirmative evaluation. The blueprint may be modified as new inputs surface or context and other variables change.
- *Do* involves collecting quantitative and qualitative data from records, individuals, or groups. The output is a report of the findings and documentation of the collection process.
- *Analyze* includes analyzing and interpreting the findings and reporting the results.
- *Improve* refers to using the results of the confirmative evaluation to make action decisions for continuous quality improvement of the learners, business, group, organization, or global community.

Chapters Three through Seven in this book discuss how to select and use soft and hard technology to accomplish each event in the confirmative evaluation process: plan, do, analyze, and improve. Soft technology can improve the effectiveness of the confirmative evaluation process; hard technologies help get the job done with maximum efficiency and help to sell confirmative evaluation as an opportunity to validate continuous improvement despite the added costs. Computer and video teleconferencing; Internet, intranet, and other communication networks; information and knowledge systems; groupware; and other software resources for flowcharting, process mapping, project management, statistical processes, multimedia presentations, and desktop publishing greatly expand the potential for widespread information mining, analysis, storage, retrieval, and communication.

Outputs of Confirmative Evaluation

Outputs are "whatever the system is producing and entering into its environment" (Banathy, 1991, p. 189) or "the aggregated products of the system which are delivered or deliverable . . ." (Kaufman, Rojas, and Mayer, 1993, p. 12). In an interactive system such as confirmative evaluation, the outputs of one event become the inputs for the next event and for the final outcomes. Figure 2.2 illustrates the ins and outs of confirmative evaluation.

Figure 2.2. Ins and Outs of Confirmative Evaluation.

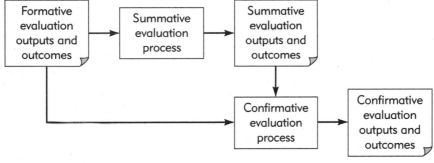

There are five major outputs of the confirmative evaluation process:

1. Confirmative evaluation plan or blueprint, including goal, timing, resources, audience, and activities

2. Data-gathering instruments

3. Documentation of the findings, both quantitative and qualitative, and the process (who, what, where, when, why, and how)

4. Analysis-based report including results, transfer, value-added components, ethical dimensions, and change drivers

5. Action decisions to maintain, revise, discard, or replace the training program

Outcomes of Confirmative Evaluation

Outcomes are the current or future ". . . effects of the outputs in and for society and the client" (Kaufman, Rojas, and Mayer, 1993, p. 12). The desired outcome of confirmative evaluation is continuous quality improvement on the part of the learners, business group, training program, organization, or global community—that is, long-term training program efficiency, effectiveness, impact, or value. As a result of confirmative evaluation, quality assurance, control, and improvement of education, training, and learning are possible because of solid and valid findings that describe the impact and value of a training program over time:

> . . . an organization that provides quality training and [that] continuously improves the way in which it produces that training, would have a quality training system that includes:
>
> - use of documented training analysis, design, development and implementation processes that result in well-defined products (quality planning),
> - use of criteria to evaluate the products and/or results of using each training process (quality control), and
> - use of procedures to review and revise training processes (quality improvement) [Dick, 1993, p. 37].

Outcomes that support continuous quality improvement of the organization may include a valued return on investment (ROI) and a positive impact on the organization's culture, market dexterity, and competitive advantage. Learner-based outcomes include continuous quality improvement of individual knowledge, skill, attitude, or performance. Confirmative evaluation outcomes may also have a number of impacts on aspects of living and working in a global community: encouraging learning organizations and workplace literacy initiatives; supporting the integration of business, personal, social, and cultural goals; and easing the transition to and the effectiveness of mega organizations and partnerships.

Example of a Follow-Up Evaluation of Learning Outcomes

Over the past decade, the American Society for Training and Development (ASTD) has worked with businesses around the globe to place a value on enterprisewide investments in workplace learning; create standards for measuring and valuing firms' investments in education and training; and link learning investments and results. The link between investments and results is established by using a combination of summative and confirmative evaluation. Enterprises that participate in the project measure and benchmark their learning outcomes at two points in time:

1. At the conclusion of the learning event, to capture the learners' immediate assessment of the usefulness of what they learned and their reaction to the training (summative evaluation)

2. Approximately three to twelve months after the learning event, to assess the usefulness of their learning over time and the effects on productivity (confirmative evaluation)

For a sample annual report of the ASTD findings, see Bassi and Ahlstrand, 2000.

Meta Evaluation Centers Confirmative Evaluation

Meta evaluation—judging the merit, worth, and value of an evaluation—is at the center of the Confirmative Evaluation Model. It completes the full-scope evaluation process by validating all evaluation processes and verifying that the evaluation outputs and outcomes are credible: "When evaluation goes wrong, the fault lies . . . not with the concept but with the way in which the evaluation is conducted. . . . The purpose of meta evaluation is to help evaluation live up to its potential" (Fitzpatrick, Sanders, and Worthen, 2004, p. 443).

Challenges to Implementing Confirmative Evaluation

Chapter One spent some time discussing generic challenges to the success of all types of evaluation (formative, summative, confirmative, and meta). Meeting these generic challenges is particularly difficult when planning and implementing confirmative evaluation; for example, the new organizations of the twenty-first century expect training and HPT departments to provide the human and other resources required to implement confirmative evaluation. This in turn will make it necessary for evaluation, training, and HPT

practitioners to acquire and use a new set of knowledge and skills and lead
to a new set of challenges specific to the implementation of confirmative
evaluation:

- Gain and maintain organizational support

- Overcome time warp factors

- Model continuous improvement

- Monitor implementation

- Conduct cost-benefit analysis (CBA) or return on investment (ROI)
  analysis when required

Gain and Maintain Organizational Support

Confirmative evaluation is not a traditional evaluation process. It may occur
over a long period of time, and long after the training program is implemented and other evaluation efforts are completed. Therefore it is especially
important to locate a champion and identify a support network that will continue to advocate for confirmative evaluation from beginning (plan) to end
(improve). The champion works closely with the practitioner, the stakeholders, and the program support network to encourage, promote, and serve their
multiple evaluation interests. The primary purpose of the support network is
to link people within the organization for sharing information resources rel-
ative to focusing, designing, and implementing the entire confirmative evaluation project.

Overcome Time Warp Factors

In a full-scope evaluation, planning for confirmative evaluation is proactive
or up-front. One time-related challenge is to develop a confirmative evaluation plan that is flexible enough to accommodate change over time. The confirmative evaluation plan must be responsive to input from all the current
stakeholders, yet flexible enough to adapt to predictable and nonpredictable
changes that may occur before the plan is implemented. When it is time to
activate the confirmative evaluation plan, the evaluation, training, or HPT

practitioner must approach it from a "That was then; what is now?" perspective. For example, over time stakeholders may change, the program may undergo revisions, and the organizational climate may change. The practitioner needs to review the original training program design document and evaluation plan to determine which stakeholders are still viable or who else needs to be involved. The evaluator must also review stakeholder needs and related evaluation outcomes. It is easier to adapt the plan to the current situation if the original plan is a systematic, thoughtful, complete, and accurate reflection of the situation at the time it was conceived.

Another time-related factor is attempting to determine the enduring value of long-term education, training, and learning. Designers and developers of long-term instructional performance support systems (such as training) need to know that their efforts have paid off—and have led to continuous improvement. Managers and other decision makers have to know that the resources expended on long-term education, training, and learning result in a positive return on investment.

Model Continuous Improvement

The purpose of confirmative evaluation is continuous improvement, and the process of confirmative evaluation should model the process of continuous improvement. The gurus of quality (Juran, Crosby, Deming, and others) all suggest guidelines for continuous improvement processes such as planning, providing feedback, monitoring or controlling, and acting on the results. These guidelines need to be incorporated into the process of planning and implementing confirmative evaluation.

One way to model continuous improvement is to plan a customer-focused confirmative evaluation that addresses these issues:

- Who are the customers, and what are their expectations?
- What processes and resources will meet the customers' expectations?
- What assessment can we make to tell us if we're meeting those expectations?
- How can we improve? (Moseley and Solomon, 1997, p. 14)

Monitor Implementation

When confirmative evaluation is part of a full-scope evaluation plan, it is helpful to monitor the training program until it is time to conduct the confirmative evaluation (for more information on monitoring, see Chapter Four). Monitoring a training program to yield input for confirmative evaluation is a challenge because it requires an ongoing, consistent effort involving time, money, and personnel. The evaluator must be flexible enough to adapt to new trends in training—for example, a change from classroom to asynchronous learning, just-in-time, or just-for-me delivery that occurs after the initial implementation and requires special evaluation strategies.

McKenzie and Smeltzer (2001) discuss three stages of program implementation that create opportunities for monitoring the training program: pilot, phased-in, and total. Monitoring the results after the program is fully implemented can be a disaster without inclusion of, and input from, pilot or phased-in monitoring activities. The evaluation, training, or HPT practitioner may need to rework desired confirmative evaluation outcomes; develop measures that compensate for a lack of prior formative and summative evaluation; or develop new tools to assess student reaction, learning, and transfer.

Conduct CBA or ROI

A true confirmative evaluation seeks to establish both the tangible and the intangible merit or worth of a training program. Sometimes money talks louder than words, though, and organizations want to know whether the training program was literally "worth it." If tangible worth is the main purpose of the confirmative evaluation, practitioners can use cost-benefit analysis (CBA) or return on investment (ROI) techniques. CBA helps determine the impact of a long-term training program by placing a monetary value on the tangible, and sometimes intangible, benefits of the training program and comparing them to the program's development and implementation costs. ROI analysis is useful for determining the value of a long-term training program by comparing the cost of designing, developing, and implementing the training program with the dollar amount of the results—for example, tangible results such as increased volume of products and services or decreased production expenses, and intangible results such as increased customer satisfaction or employee motivation.

The challenges to the evaluation, training, and HPT practitioners include:

- Selecting the right strategy
- Mastering the technical aspects of conducting a CBA or ROI analysis
- Identifying and quantifying hidden costs such as participant time away from the job
- Identifying and putting a monetary value on benefits

In the past, evaluators were expected to have the knowledge and skills required to identify the human, financial, and time costs associated with a training program (Worthen and Sanders, 1987). Today's training or HPT practitioners should also have, know where to access, or acquire this knowledge and skill set. Chapter Six presents more specific information on how to conduct a CBI or ROI analysis, including a list of additional resources.

Why Bother?

Why would an organization want to conduct a confirmative evaluation despite the challenges involved? Why bother? The answer to these questions ". . . has implications for how we measure and how we use the products of the measurement process" (Binder, 2001, p. 21). It also gives the practitioner a purpose-based rationale for planning and marketing confirmative evaluation.

Addressing evaluation in general, Geis and Smith (1992) suggest that even though the commonly accepted purpose of evaluation is decision making, evaluation should also strive to "to illuminate and improve the organization" (p. 133). Addressing the issue of improvement, Binder (2001) adds, "There are essentially three reasons for measurement in the science and practice of performance improvement: validation [of methods, procedures, programs], accountability, and decision-making" (p. 21).

The needs of stakeholders become the purposes that initiate a confirmative evaluation. Stakeholders may need to verify accountability, support a decision, validate success, establish professional credibility, or respond to a trigger event (such as the need to determine whether a training program is in compliance with new health and safety or quality standards). The rule of thumb is to pick a purpose for the confirmative evaluation that aligns with the organization's mission, values, goals, and culture.

Verify Accountability

The term *accountability* implies responsibility for results (Ghattas and McKee, 2001, pp. 60–61). Decision makers chart the course of action and may or may not supervise the confirmative process. Those who do make the decisions and are responsible for the successful implementation of the training program share accountability for the results and need to be open to self-assessment or external assessment of their stewardship. Is the program still valid? Are the practice exercises still meaningful? Are the survey questions still appropriate? Can learners still perform adequately? Can the practitioner still continue to be licensed?

Assessing accountability is particularly important in technical and certification training. For example, Kemp and Cochern (1994), in their book on planning technical training, tell trainers that ". . . unbiased, objective evidence can help you decide whether the need initially recognized has been satisfied. Furthermore, in the important legal climate that is widespread in our society, your liability for properly training and then certifying student competence would be protected if there is clear evidence of the success of your instruction" (p. 163). Moseley and Solomon (1997) also suggest that "eventually, we will all be accountable for results, and confirmative evaluation will be a necessary part of every consultant's tool kit" (p. 14). Accountability has a price, however. Learning professionals must become business, financial, and organizational sophisticates in order to justify their efforts (Spitzer, 2002).

Support Decision Making

Binder (2001) writes: "For scientists, technologists, and professionals in many fields, a principal purpose for measurement is to support decisions about what to do next, how to adjust procedures, or when to make changes. . . . decision making is the *highest purpose for measurement,* and it generally subsumes the other two purposes [validation and accountability]" (p. 21). Decision makers may use the results of confirmative evaluation to improve training programs, organizations, or the global community in which the organization functions. At the program level, the decision maker has the option to maintain, revise, discard, or replace the training program with an existing or new delivery system. At the organization or global level, the decision maker may choose either action or planned nonaction. If action wins out, the decision maker must also choose the best options for implementing and managing the changes required to ensure success.

In the current global business environment, the confirmative evaluation outcome data that are most important for driving or supporting decision making are organizational impact data, cost-benefit ratio data, and ROI data. Geis and Smith (1992, p. 133) conclude that there is a direct relationship between the degree to which the purpose of an evaluation is "explicit, specific, and detailed" and how smoothly the evaluation activities unfold.

Validate Success

Given the new organization of the twenty-first century, it is becoming more and more important for evaluation, training, and HPT practitioners to be able to verify that what they said would happen has really happened. Even a decade ago, Carr (1992, p. 149) wrote this advice to an audience of training and other managers: "If your training department (or training consultant) follows a solid analysis, design, and development process, the training will improve performance. As managers, though, . . . we have to follow up to see that the training, in fact, was successful." More recently, Watkins and Kaufman (2002) suggest that two critical elements for organizational success from a management perspective are "selecting effective and efficient [performance] interventions (that is, processes, activities, training programs) and the continuous improvement of existing interventions" (p. 24). The outcomes of confirmative evaluation validate both the effectiveness and the efficiency of the instructional or noninstructional performance intervention and the value of the intervention in terms of continuous improvement.

Establish Professional Credibility

Measurement of results is *essential* to the professional practice of performance improvement through training. In today's business environment, training is a business and it is increasingly important to establish the *business value* of any performance intervention, including training. Measuring the behavior, work outputs (accomplishments), and business results we seek to improve helps training and HPT practitioners validate results and develop powerful, credible business cases for themselves and their programs (Binder, 2002b, 2002c; Spitzer, 2002). Without measurement, our technology lacks empirical foundation and our claims lack credibility.

Respond to Trigger Events

Certain events may trigger the need for including confirmative evaluation in the evaluation plan for a new training program or designing confirmative evaluation for an established program that has been in existence for years or decades. The trigger event may reflect existing or changed needs in any of a number of areas: political outlook, priorities of the organization or the global community, problem scope, severity, effectiveness, efficiency, resource availability, or regulatory requirements (Rossi and Freeman, 1993). Responding to a trigger event may appear less desirable than an up-front desire to validate improved performance or support decision making, but the results of the confirmative evaluation may still have a profound impact on the organization, and there are the same issues to confront: Should we include confirmative evaluation in the training evaluation plan? How do we obtain support for confirmative evaluation within the organization?

SUMMARY: LESSONS LEARNED IN CHAPTER TWO

1. The Confirmative Evaluation Model illustrates that confirmative evaluation is a systematic, concept-based, iterative process with inputs, processes, outputs, and outcomes.

2. Aligning the purpose with organization mission, values, goals, climate, and culture helps to sell confirmative evaluation to decision makers.

3. In addition to the challenges associated with evaluation in general, evaluation, training, and HPT practitioners face specific challenges as they plan to implement confirmative evaluation.

4. Most organizations "bother" with confirmative evaluation because they want to validate that a training program really improved performance, or they need to support decision making.

5. Personal lessons learned:

_____

_____

_____

_____

_____

_____

_____

NEXT STEPS

Part Two discusses the confirmative evaluation process events illustrated in the Moseley-Dessinger Confirmative Evaluation Model—*plan, do, analyze, improve*—including the inputs, process, outputs, and outcomes of each event.

PART 2

Meeting the Challenge

From evaluability assessment to continuous improvement, evaluation, training, and HPT practitioners *plan, do, analyze,* and *improve.* A Toolbox of additional resources at the end of each chapter helps practitioners plan and implement a successful confirmative evaluation.

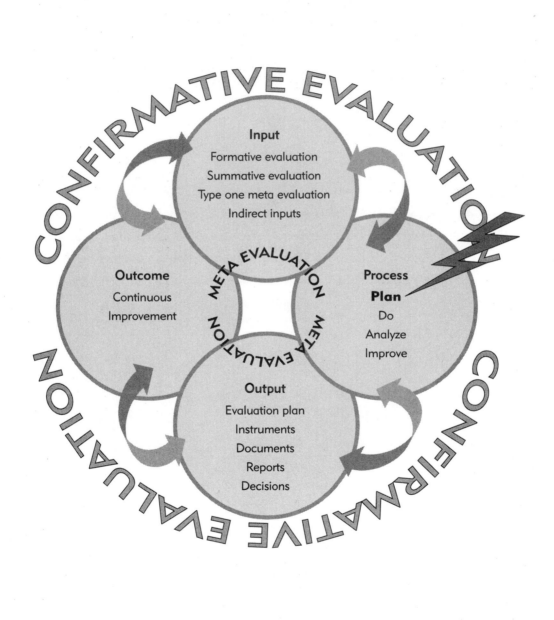

CONFIRMATIVE EVALUATION

Input
Formative evaluation
Summative evaluation
Type one meta evaluation
Indirect inputs

Outcome
Continuous
Improvement

META EVALUATION

META EVALUATION

Process
Plan
Do
Analyze
Improve

Output
Evaluation plan
Instruments
Documents
Reports
Decisions

CONFIRMATIVE EVALUATION

3

Preplan: Assess Training Program Evaluability

CHAPTERS THREE AND FOUR are all about planning, the first step in the process component of our Confirmative Evaluation Model. The approach we take to planning evaluation is reinforced throughout the literature (Smith and Brandenburg, 1991; Shrock and Geis, 1999; and others). Our "P⁴" motto is simple: prior planning prevents problems, and it helps ensure success.

In Chapters Three and Four, we also assume that an evaluation, training, or HPT practitioner is in place to direct and guide the confirmative evaluation process. This HPT practitioner is the logical person to guide confirmative evaluation planning activities, or at the very least take an active role in all the planning and implementation activities. A practitioner should possess:

- Theoretical and practical knowledge of evaluation

- Ability to use hard and soft technology to maximize the efficiency, effectiveness, and validity of the confirmative evaluation process

- Project management skills to complete the evaluation in time and on budget, and to produce a final report that meets the needs of all stakeholders (see Chapter Four)

- Awareness of any ethical and political implications and the ability to exercise judgments in thinking and decision making that are ethically and politically sound

The role of the practitioner as director or guide does not downplay the need for collaboration in planning and conducting confirmative evaluation. Rossman and Rallis (2000) suggest that the practitioner and the stakeholders should be viewed as *partners and coproducers of knowledge* because "both partners are essential to questioning assumptions, collecting data, making meaning, generating alternatives, and finally, to using information . . ." (p. 67).

Chapter Three reviews the planning process and zooms in on the first activity in the process, the preplanning stage or assessing program evaluability. We begin by discussing the importance of differentiating whether the planning is proactive (up-front) or reactive (just-in-time). Then we present our blended approach to planning confirmative evaluation and offer guidelines for conducting a training program evaluability assessment. We conclude with some of the challenges associated with evaluability assessment.

After reading this chapter, you will be able to:

1. Recognize the benefits and drawbacks of proactive and reactive planning

2. Identify the major activities involved in planning confirmative evaluation

3. Explain why confirmative evaluation planners should preplan a confirmative evaluation by assessing the evaluability of the training program

4. Use performance support tools to assess the evaluability of a training program

5. Recognize the challenges to planning confirmative evaluation

When to Plan Confirmative Evaluation

Planning for confirmative evaluation may take place up front (proactive) or just in time (reactive). There are benefits and drawbacks associated with initiating both proactive and reactive planning. Table 3.1 compares proactive and reactive planning for confirmative evaluation in terms of three factors: timeliness, integration, and resources.

Table 3.1. Proactive or Reactive Planning for Confirmative Evaluation?

	Proactive (Up-Front) Planning	Reactive (Just-in-Time) Planning
Timeliness	Changes may occur during the one-year or longer lapse between planning and implementation of confirmative evaluation: • Stakeholders and stakeholders' needs • Training program revisions • Organizational structure and climate • Other . . .	Planning takes place just prior to confirmative evaluation and is based on current situation: • Stakeholder needs • Training program version • Organizational structure and climate • Other . . .
Integration	Inputs, process, outputs, and outcomes for full-scope evaluation—formative, summative, confirmative, and meta—are integrated into the up-front training program plan	Existing data from formative and summative evaluation may or may not: • Be available • Support stakeholder information needs • Support desired confirmative evaluation outcomes
Resources	Time lapse between planning and implementing confirmative evaluation requires extra time and other resources to: • Monitor training program • Maintain (review, revise, approve) confirmative evaluation plan	Immediate implementation of confirmative evaluation plan does not require additional time and other resources for monitoring and maintaining

Proactive Planning

Proactive or up-front planning for evaluation occurs during the *analyze, design,* and sometimes *develop* phases of the ADDIE model for instructional design. Parkman links proactive planning for evaluation to training or performance needs analysis and suggests these benefits:

- It ensures that the (evaluation) projects you undertake will have real value.
- It forces you to clarify your goals in terms of the business results you want to impact and the job performance changes you need to make.
- It ensures that the solutions you implement are based on data, not intuition.
- It helps to secure needed buy-in from key stakeholders who will be instrumental in helping you complete your analysis.
- It provides meaningful data for use in comparing pre- and post-intervention performance.
- It enhances the credibility of your results [2002, n. p.]

Proactive planning also means that planners can integrate the needs of all the types of evaluation (formative, summative, confirmative, and meta) into one full-scope plan. In addition, proactive planning "coordinates and consolidates needs assessment and evaluation where possible, which saves time and money . . . streamlines the process . . . and helps improve collaboration" among the evaluation, training, or HPT practitioner and stakeholders (Korth, 2001, pp. 39, 43). The potential drawback is the need to be flexible because of the time lapse between planning and conducting confirmative evaluation.

Reactive Planning

Reactive or just-in-time planning takes place months or even years after a training program is implemented and focuses on confirmative evaluation or type two meta evaluation. Reactive planning is usually triggered by a request from a stakeholder for information about the efficiency, effectiveness, impact, or value of a training program after the program has been in existence for an extended period of time. The benefit of reactive planning is that there is no time lapse between planning and implementing the confirmative evaluation, so the plan is current and immediate. The drawback is the lack of integration with formative and summative evaluation.

Movement Toward Proactive Planning?

There are some indications of movement toward proactive planning. Lynn Schmidt writes: "HRD organizations today have to be accountable, justify expenditures, demonstrate performance improvement, deliver results based training, improve processes, and be proactive. Utilizing measurement and evaluation tools in HRD organizations is no longer a reactive decision. The leaders of HRD organizations realize that business leaders are expecting to see results for the dollars invested in training and they are proactively measuring the results of training initiatives" (2002, n. p.).

One example of the movement toward proactive planning is Spitzer's Super Evaluation. Lindsley reported in 1999 that ". . . Spitzer's Super-Evaluation is usually done entirely after the fact . . . [however] he suggests that the very first thing to be done in starting a project is to select the project's desired impact on the organization and use evaluation to mold the project to that desired outcome instead of simply using evaluation to assess consequences at the end" (p. 211). Spitzer and Conway (2002) have since evolved Super Evaluation into a model called Training Results Measurement (TRM) and suggest using the model up front to design results-oriented training programs.

How to Plan a Confirmative Evaluation

The activities involved in planning a successful confirmative evaluation are basically the same as the activities for planning any type of program evaluation. For example, Smith and Brandenburg (1991) suggest an eight-step planning process that emphasizes using input from decision makers to design and document an evaluation plan that takes into account current constraints, resources, and opportunities.

Blended Approach

After reading the literature, we have developed a blended approach to planning confirmative evaluation. Our approach emphasizes these keys to being successful:

- Assess the evaluability of the training program up front
- Stress the crucial role of stakeholders as decision makers and planners
- Develop a confirmative evaluation plan that is complete (who, what, where, when, why, and how), accurate, flexible, credible, and useful
- Use evaluation outcomes to improve performance

The blended approach adapts to both proactive and reactive planning.

Planning Process Flow

PST 3.1 is a guide to using the blended planning process. The process is composed of several activities, tasks, and major decision points:

- Activities:

    Assess evaluability

    Develop the confirmative evaluation plan
- Tasks:

    Assess the program

    Assess needs

    Assess outcomes

    Develop the plan

    Maintain the plan (proactive planning only)
- Decisions:

    Is the training program evaluable?

    Are all stakeholder needs evaluable?

    Are the evaluation outcomes evaluable?

    Do stakeholders commit to action or nonaction?

    Is the plan approved?

PST 3.1. Confirmative Evaluation Planning Process Flowchart.

Purpose of this PST: To guide the evaluation, training, or HPT practitioner through the confirmative evaluation process.

How to use this PST: Use this flowchart as a process map. Just begin with box one and follow the arrows. Make sure that you involve as many stakeholders as possible whenever you reach a decision point (diamond).

Note: If the response to three of the decision questions (program evaluable? outcomes evaluable? plan approved?) is no, you have two options for action: reassess or revise the plan or decide not to conduct a confirmative evaluation (commit to nonaction) and end the planning session.

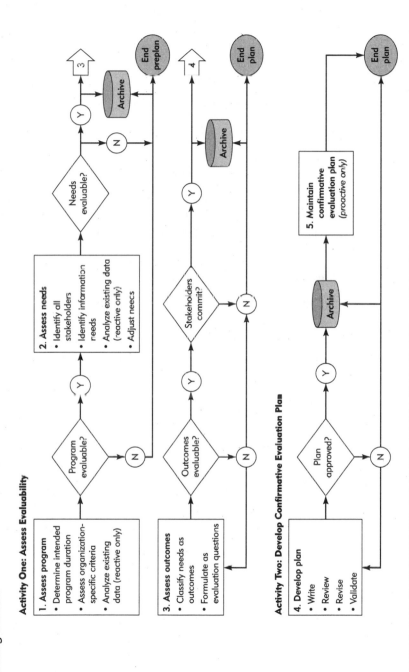

Confirmative Evaluation: Practical Strategies for Valuing Continuous Improvement. Copyright © 2004 by John Wiley & Sons, Inc. Reproduced by permission of Pfeiffer, an Imprint of Wiley. www.pfeiffer.com

Tasks vary depending on whether the planning is proactive or reactive. Both proactive and reactive planning begin by assessing the evaluability of the training program, according to the intended duration of the program, organization-specific criteria related to the program, and stakeholder information needs. Reactive planners also review existing formative and summative evaluation data and analyze whether there is a gap between existing data and stakeholder needs. A gap could have an impact on the evaluability of stakeholder needs or make it necessary to adjust the needs.

Once the evaluation outcomes are assessed and validated as evaluable, and once the stakeholders commit to acting on the outcomes to improve performance, both proactive and reactive planners develop the confirmative evaluation plan and initiate a review-approve-validate cycle for the plan. Reactive planners then implement the plan while proactive planners maintain the plan, making revisions as needed until it is time to begin the confirmative evaluation.

Throughout both proactive and reactive planning, the practitioner should document and archive the inputs, process, outputs, and outcomes of the planning process. Documents archived in the appropriate knowledge, information, or training management system are available to current and future evaluation planners and are useful for justifying decisions and communicating with all the stakeholders.

Assess Evaluability

Wholey (1994), who first used the term *evaluability* in the 1970s, offers a rationale for beginning evaluation planning with evaluability assessment: "Rather than having the evaluator construct an evaluation design that may prove to be irrelevant, infeasible, inconclusive, untimely, or otherwise useless . . . evaluability assessment begins the evaluation planning process by carrying out a preliminary assessment of the program design" (p. 17). Shrock and Geis (1999) draw a parallel between evaluability assessment and front-end analysis, emphasizing that despite the outcomes of the evaluability assessment, ". . . deciding to do a different evaluation, or not to do an evaluation at all [inaction], should remain a valid option during the planning stage" (p. 197).

There are three major tasks related to evaluability assessment: (1) assess the program, that is, the intended duration, organization-specific criteria, and existing data (reactive only); (2) assess stakeholder needs, that is, identify stakeholders and assess their information needs; and (3) assess outcomes; that is, classify needs as outcomes and formulate as evaluation questions.

PST 3.2 is a performance support tool that is useful for determining whether to conduct a confirmative evaluation of a specific training program. This PST helps the practitioner record and rate the outcome data related to intended program duration, organization-specific criteria, and stakeholder information needs. For reactive planners, there is also a section for assessing existing data.

PST 3.2. Confirmative Evaluation Evaluability Assessment Form for Training Programs.

Purpose of this PST: Determine whether it is appropriate to conduct a confirmative evaluation of a training program.

How to use this PST:

1. Use some or all of the items below, or fill in your own evaluability factors.

2. Make sure each item has the same meaning for all respondents (for example, in item six you need to determine the accepted interpretation of "well-defined" goals and objectives).

3. Ask training program stakeholders to rate each item in each category.

4. Rule of thumb: If a majority of the stakeholders rate 80 percent or more of the items in a category (an example is training program intended duration) as very true or true, then the program is evaluable within that category.

Rating key: 4 = Very true   3 = True   2 = Not always true   1 = Untrue

Name of Training Program:

Training Program Intended Duration	Rating (4–1)
1. Intended program duration is one to five or more years.	
2. Intended program duration is less than one year, but certification or licensing requirements mandate a confirmative evaluation.	
3. Intended program duration is less than one year, but stakeholder requests an extension.	
4. Other:	
5. Other:	
Organization-Specific Criteria	
6. Program goals and objectives are well defined.	
7. Program goals and objectives are achievable.	
8. Program goals and objectives align with business goals.	

PST 3.2. Confirmative Evaluation Evaluability Assessment Form for Training Programs, *Continued*.

Rating key: 4 = Very true   3 = True   2 = Not always true   1 = Untrue

	Rating (4–1)
9. Program goals are critical to meeting organizational goals.	
10. Program goals and objectives are consistent with organizational or business goals and objectives.	
11. Priority needs of training audience are well defined.	
12. Training program development and implementation budget is large.	
13. Size of the training audience is large.	
14. Training audience represents a critical business area or areas.	
15. Training program is very visible internally or externally.	
16. Organization has the resource capability (time, expertise, technology, money, and so forth) to support a confirmative evaluation.	
17. Management is very interested in evaluating the training program.	
18. Other:	
19. Other:	

Stakeholder-Information Needs

20. All stakeholders are identified.	
21. All stakeholders provided input.	
22. Stakeholder information needs are identified.	
23. Stakeholder needs are critical to achieving work group goals.	
24. Stakeholder needs are critical to achieving business and organization goals.	
25. Stakeholder information needs are evaluable (clear, useful, measurable).	

PST 3.2. Confirmative Evaluation Evaluability Assessment Form for Training Programs, *Continued*.

Rating key: 4 = Very true   3 = True   2 = Not always true   1 = Untrue

	Rating (4–1)
26. Evaluation outcomes are well defined.	
27. Evaluation outcomes are evaluable (clear, useful, measurable).	
28. Stakeholders will use evaluation outcomes to improve performance.	
29. Other:	
30. Other:	
Support from Existing Data (Reactive Planning Only)	
31. Existing formative and summative evaluation data assess current organization-specific criteria.	
32. Existing formative and summative evaluation data meet all of the stakeholders' information needs.	
33. Data are missing, but it is possible to assess organization-specific criteria without the missing data.	
34. Data are missing, but it is possible to meet stakeholder information needs without the missing data.	
35. Missing data are retrievable.	
36. We can collect missing data through confirmative evaluation.	
37. We do not need to assess the organization-specific criteria not covered by existing data.	
38. We can adjust stakeholder needs to adjust for missing data.	
39. Other:	
40. Other:	

Assess the Program

There are three subtasks involved in assessing the evaluability of the training program. The practitioner determines the intended program duration, assesses organization-specific criteria, and, if the confirmative planning is reactive, analyzes existing data. Only then is it possible to decide whether the training program is evaluable.

Determine Intended Program Duration. The first step in assessing evaluability is to determine how long the training program is scheduled to continue. Confirmative evaluation is appropriate when the intended training program duration is one year or longer. Occasionally, special requirements may dictate the need to conduct a confirmative evaluation of a short-term (or even one-time-only) program. An example of that need is when accreditation, certification, licensing, oversight, or compliance requirements mandate confirmative evaluation even if the program runs for less than one year. Another instance would be if stakeholders ask the training department to extend the duration of a short-term or one-time-only training program and the training department needs confirmative evaluation data to support or deny the request.

PST 3.2 suggests how to rate the evaluability of a training program in terms of intended duration factors.

Assess Organization-Specific Criteria. The second step in evaluability assessment is to gather and review organization-specific criteria for the training program. Organization-specific criteria may include internal standards for designing, implementing, and evaluating a training program as well as criteria related to participant and other reactions, cost-benefit ratio, return on investment, and other factors. Ideally, evaluation, training, or HPT departments identify and include organization-specific criteria as part of the department's documented evaluation protocol. If criteria do not exist, the practitioner may need to identify stakeholders and then generate the criteria with the help of the stakeholders. PST 3.2 suggests some generic criteria to jump-start this process.

Criteria are often based on individual needs, concerns, and perceptions. When stakeholders are involved, it is imperative that they all agree on a common meaning for each criterion (Smith, 1989). Once criteria are generated, the practitioner may record them on PST 3.2 and use the form to rate the evaluability of a training program.

Analyze Existing Data. Existing data are quite useful for assessing evaluability and identifying organization-specific criteria. Data on the training program itself are not available if the confirmative evaluation is planned up front (proactive planning). However, there may be information on generic organization-specific criteria that could prove helpful for establishing what the organization expects from the program in terms of outputs and outcomes.

Reactive planners have the added opportunity to analyze existing formative or summative evaluation data. The purpose of this analysis is to determine if information exists that helps determine (1) whether organization-specific criteria were taken into account when the training program was designed and developed, and if so then (2) whether documentation supports how well the program outcomes met the criteria. Any gaps between organization-specific criteria then and now, or any gaps in reporting outcomes related to the criteria then and now, are identified and the practitioner can determine whether it is possible to use confirmative evaluation to bridge these gaps.

Decision Time: Is Program Evaluable? The first decision point is equivalent to an early warning system or yellow flag; it applies program-duration and organization-specific criteria to the training program even before process planning begins. If the training program is not long-term or does not meet 80 percent of the organization-specific criteria, then the evaluator may suggest that it is not appropriate to conduct a confirmative evaluation. However, if there is an overriding political or other need for confirmative evaluation, the practitioner may continue the planning process by identifying the stakeholders and assessing their information needs.

Assess Needs

There are three to four subtasks involved in assessing stakeholder needs. First, the practitioner identifies all the potential stakeholders. Then the practitioner identifies stakeholder information needs, analyzes existing data (if the planning is reactive), and helps the stakeholder adjust their needs if necessary. At this point it is possible to decide whether stakeholder needs are evaluable.

Identify All Stakeholders. Assessing information needs involves identifying all the stakeholders and assessing what information they need that will help them improve performance or make decisions. Stakeholders are ". . . organizations and people who are involved in or affected by the performance and results of a program" (Boulmetis and Dutwin, 2000, p. 23). Stakeholders may include program participants, sponsors, and staff, as well as external or internal customers, decision makers, and others who are affected by the program outcomes. Lipps and Grant (1990) write that involving stakeholders and internal professionals, such as evaluators, training staff, HPT staff, analysts, subject experts, and others, in the confirmative evaluation planning process helps identify constraints, drive modifications to the plan, create buy-in from the organization, and improve the feedback process.

Look for the Decision Makers. Many stakeholders are decision makers. For example, some may use the evaluation outcomes to decide whether to retain, revise, reject, or replace the training program, or use evaluation outcomes to improve performance within their work group or business or throughout the organization. Worthen, Sanders, and Fitzpatrick (1997) show an example of a matrix (on p. 218) that lists potential stakeholders in one column and uses a series of check-off columns to match each stakeholder to a specific type of decision (for example, operational decision, policy decision, marketing decision, and so forth).

Don't Forget a Champion. While identifying stakeholders, it is important to remember that every confirmative evaluation needs a champion. A champion is a visionary who recognizes and supports the need for change, believes in the philosophy and practice of confirmative evaluation, is able to visualize and articulate value-added benefits, knows how to establish relationships and build a climate of trust, understands organizational realities, is able to garner political and financial support, and overcomes obstacles to confirmative thinking (Daft, 1997).

The evaluation, training, or HPT practitioner has several options for selecting a champion, using whatever technologies (virtual, telecommunications, computer) are available and accepted within the organization:

- Ask the training program champion to promote the confirmative evaluation or suggest a champion
- Ask the person who requested the confirmative evaluation to be the champion or suggest one
- Select a champion from the training program stakeholders
- Ask colleagues and stakeholders for suggestions
- Select a champion from among the high-profile individuals within the organization

Clarify Stakeholder Expectations. During the stakeholder identification process, the evaluator needs to clarify and communicate clear and realistic expectations regarding the planning roles and responsibilities of a stakeholder. For example, Is the stakeholder's responsibility limited to approving a process? piloting a procedure? making a policy decision? If the organizational climate encourages collaboration, the evaluator may negotiate the roles and responsibilities individually or on a group basis. Whatever the limitations on responsibility, shared accountability for identifying and using the outcomes of the confirmative evaluation is a given: ". . . I believe trainers and consultants have done themselves a disservice by assuming responsibility for evaluation. . . . We are responsible for the integrity of our work and products; however, the client must share the accountability for results" (Hale, 2002a, p. 1).

Time for a Reality Check. Ideally, the confirmative evaluation planning process should include everyone who has an interest in the outcomes of the training program, especially those who are responsible for using the outcome measures to improve performance. The usefulness of the evaluation outcomes is "enhanced by broad participation . . . and shared ownership of the process" (Shrock and Geis, 1999, p. 189). However, everyone may not be available at the same time. If major decision makers are ready and willing to help with the planning, then the evaluation, training, or HPT practitioners may decide to proceed with the evaluability assessment and bring additional stakeholders on board as they are identified.

Identify Information Needs. Once during an international teleconference sponsored by Ford Motor, the audience asked quality and management gurus Peter Senge and W. Edwards Deming a number of questions that focused on how to gather information from employees, board members, and so forth. Senge's answers varied, but Deming's reply was always the same: "Ask them!"

The best way to identify stakeholders' information needs is to ask them. It is vital that all stakeholders have an opportunity to articulate and share their information needs early in the planning process. The evaluation, training, or HPT practitioners may "ask them" through virtual or face-to-face interviews, questionnaires, surveys, brainstorming, or focus groups. In a collaborative environment, needs negotiation is an effective way to generate and prioritize information needs from a variety of stakeholders.

Needs Negotiation. The process of needs negotiation during instructional development is described in Coleman, Perry, and Schwen (1997, pp. 274–275) as "a search for the beliefs and values of the clients, learners, and others who have a stake in the situation . . ." Needs negotiation is especially useful for identifying the information needs of confirmative evaluation stakeholders because there are many stakeholders; each one has his or her own information need; and each information need reflects a different set of personal and organizational assumptions, values, and perspectives.

Needs *negotiation* has its roots in the constructivist approach to learning and instruction. Using needs negotiation to identify stakeholder information needs helps the stakeholders, as well as the practitioner, decide whether to conduct a confirmative evaluation. The process also generates a negotiated list of stakeholder information needs to use as a basis for developing evaluation outcomes and questions.

The evaluation, training, or HPT practitioner uses whatever technology is available, accessible, and accepted to facilitate the needs negotiation session(s). This may range from real-time meeting technologies such as flipcharts and electronic whiteboards to virtual communication technologies such as e-mail, electronic bulletin boards, chat rooms, teleconferencing, or videoconferencing. Individual interviews are another alternative; however, they are not as effective as group sessions.

Needs negotiation acknowledges the important role of the practitioner as a needs negotiator, while making the stakeholders ultimately accountable for the outcomes. PST 3.3 lists the basic steps in conducting a successful needs negotiation to generate a list of stakeholder information needs.

PST 3.3. Steps in Negotiating Stakeholder Information Needs.

Purpose: To help the evaluation, training, or HPT practitioner use needs negotiation techniques to identify, share, and accept stakeholder information needs.

Directions: The stakeholders who are involved in planning a confirmative evaluation plan have many and differing information needs. Use this group process to help the stakeholders articulate and share their needs, and develop a list of information needs that truly represent their assumptions, perspectives, and values. (You may conduct individual interviews, but the group process is more effective.)

If you want to do a self-assessment of the needs negotiation process, write one of these symbols in the blank next to each step as it is completed:

✓ Step completed successfully

X Skipped this step

? There was a problem that may have affected the result of this step

___ 1. Ask yourself these questions and record your responses: Do I feel that a confirmative evaluation is needed? Why? Why not? What information needs do I think will (or should) surface during this session?

___ 2. Ask all the stakeholders the same questions. You or the stakeholders may record the results.

___ 3. Facilitate a discussion of all the responses. Focus on comparing the various perspectives, values, and assumptions. Record the results.

___ 4. Develop a list of information needs that represent the needs of all the stakeholders.

___ 5. Use the list of information needs as the basis for deciding whether to conduct a confirmative evaluation. If the decision is yes, the document also provides a list of stakeholder needs to use as a basis for developing evaluation outcomes and questions.

Dialogue. Applying the principles of Dialogue can also enhance the process of identifying and clarifying stakeholder information needs. Dialogue increases ". . . the capacity of members of a team to suspend assumptions and enter into a genuine 'thinking together'" (Senge, 1990, p. 10). Wilson (2002) writes that dialogue is all about "how much time (you) spend in the other person's frame of reference compared to how much you spend in your own" (n.p.). Patterson, Grenny, McMillan, and Swizler (2000, p. 7) believe that dialogue is "better than duct tape" because it is capable of *fixing* just about anything dealing with human relationships at home, work, or play.

Dialogue goes beyond discussion and requires a different set of skills (Tracey, Solomon, and Moseley, unpublished manuscript). PST 3.4 suggests several Dialogue skills that the evaluation, training, or HPT practitioners may apply to enhance the needs negotiation process.

PST 3.4. Good-Better-Best Dialogue.

Purpose: To help you self-assess your personal dialogue skills or assess a dialogue interaction.

Directions for assessing your dialogue skills: Read each item below and place a ✓ in the blank next to the skill(s) you need to improve. Try to work on improvement before you begin a dialogue interaction.

Directions for assessing a dialogue interaction: During or after the dialogue interaction, put an X in the blank next to any item that is causing (or has caused) you concern. After the dialogue, ask yourself: Why was this a concern? What really happened? What do I need to do to improve the next dialogue session?

___ 1. Am I able to (did I) put aside my assumptions, values, and personal perspective and recognize or accept the other person's perspective?

___ 2. Am I able to (did I) share and clarify why I feel the way I do?

___ 3. Am I able to (did I) suspend the whole notion that one of us is right and one of us is wrong?

___ 4. Am I able to (did I) bite my tongue and not force the other person to agree or disagree with me?

___ 5. Am I able to (did I) use clarifying questions to make sure I understand the other person and he or she understands me?

___ 6. Am I able to (did I) rephrase what the other person said in my own words so I demonstrate that I understand what he or she is telling me?

Source: Based on Tracey, Solomon, and Moseley (unpublished manuscript).

Analyze Existing Evaluation Data. Once more, reactive planners have the added opportunity to analyze existing formative or summative evaluation outcome data. The purpose of the analysis is to determine whether there is a gap between current stakeholder information needs and existing data. If a gap does exist, the practitioner may find that it is necessary to adjust stakeholder needs because they have already been met by existing data, data are not available to meet their needs, or confirmative evaluation will meet their needs.

Adjust Stakeholder Needs. The practitioner may find it necessary to guide the stakeholders through needs adjustment. For example, stakeholder A wants to find out how well participants from his business performed during training. The evaluator knows that the stakeholder needs to assess participant test scores from the training program; the scores are not available, but she does have access to content outlines and performance objectives from the program and has access to or can generate workplace performance data. The evaluation, training, or HPT practitioner suggests that the stakeholder could refocus on whether the participants applied their new knowledge or skills in the workplace. Knowing when and how to suggest a needs adjustment comes from formal training or education in evaluation theory, lots of practice, networking with colleagues, and professional development activities.

Are Information Needs Evaluable? Once stakeholder information needs are negotiated or adjusted, the practitioner and the stakeholders should decide whether the needs are evaluable—that is, whether they are clear, useful, and measurable and whether data exist or may be generated to meet the information needs. PST 3.2 suggests how to rate the evaluability of stakeholder information needs.

The practitioner is responsible for helping the stakeholders refine their needs statements until they are clear (explicit and unambiguous). The key is to select a needs identification technique, such as needs negotiation, that includes opportunities to discuss and clarify individual needs.

The stakeholders, guided by the practitioner, have the primary responsibility for establishing usefulness. In his discussion of *utilization-focused evaluation,* Patton (1997, p. 23) warns that judging the merit and worth of a training program is not "an end in itself"; it is more important to identify why the stakeholder needs to know and how he or she will use the information. Ultimately, stakeholder information needs should align with current business and organization needs, which in turn align with long-term business and organization goals.

The practitioner has the primary responsibility for determining whether stakeholder needs are measurable using standard quantitative or qualitative techniques. The evaluator validates measurability once the needs are formulated as evaluation outcomes.

Assess Outcomes

Stakeholder information needs may surface as questions, concerns, statements of fact or perception, or random thoughts. Stakeholders are generally not trained to think like evaluators; they may not know what evaluation can do for them. The evaluation, training, or HPT practitioner should help the stakeholders formulate evaluation outcomes by classifying their needs in such terms and then writing evaluation questions.

Classify Needs as Outcomes. The term *program evaluation outcome* refers to the cause-and-effect relationship between training program activities and their expected, measurable results: "Outcomes are what occur as a direct result of an action" (Boulmetis and Dutwin, 2000, p. 25). The traditional outcomes that stakeholders look for at the end of confirmative evaluation are efficiency and effectiveness. Impact and value are often folded into the discussion of effectiveness; however, we suggest that impact and value are outcomes in their own right and should be treated separately.

Efficiency. If the stakeholders need to know whether the benefits of a training program are greater than the time and cost of program development and implementation, they are asking whether the program is efficient. Evaluation experts generally agree that efficiency refers to ". . . the degree to which a program or project has been productive in relationship to its resources" (Boulmetis and Dutwin, 2000, p. 3).

Effectiveness. If stakeholders want to know whether their repair technicians learned how to troubleshoot a new product or were able to apply their new troubleshooting knowledge in the field, the stakeholders want to know whether the training program was effective. Most evaluation experts are in agreement that effectiveness deals with program goals and "the degree to which goals have been reached" (Boulmetis and Dutwin, 2000, p. 3). For example, Carr (1992) writes, "Effectiveness means that training improves performance as much as possible" (p. 136).

Some experts, including Carr (1992), suggest that impact and value are elements of effectiveness. However, we prefer to view impact and value as separate outcomes of confirmative evaluation.

Impact. If the stakeholders need to know whether a training program helped a business unit improve quality, decrease cycle time, or increase customer satisfaction, they are asking about the impact of the training program: "According to estimates from ASTD and others, only 3 percent of all training courses are evaluated for business impact" (Spitzer, 2002, p. 1).

As a stand-alone outcome, impact is the degree to which a training program results in intended performance improvement over time. For example, Boulmetis and Dutwin (2000) refer to impact as "the degree to which a program or project resulted in [positive or negative] change" (p. 3). They offer this example: "Longer range, more sustained results [outcomes] of an action may be termed 'impacts,' which need to be measured after a period to allow for things to percolate and settle in. For example, a training program may be deemed effective, given the impressive outcomes after its completion. However, within three months, due to lack of retention or lack of use or 'buy-in,' the new knowledge has not been put to use in the work place. Thus there was little or no impact from the training" (p. 25).

The terms *training for impact* (Robinson, 1984; Robinson and Robinson, 1989) and *training for results* (Brinkerhoff, 1987; Brinkerhoff and Apking, 2001) imply that impact is the intended outcome of a training program. Robinson and Robinson (1989) state that impact training is "needs-driven," "results-oriented," and "applicable to any situation where training's purpose is to help the organization achieve its objectives" (p. 11).

Training program results may have an impact on individuals, groups, or the whole organization; policies, procedures, or products; systems, standards, or services. For example, Kirkpatrick (1994) defines his fourth and last level of evaluation as ". . . the final results that occurred because the participants attended the program. The final results can include increased production, improved quality, decreased costs, reduced frequency and/or severity of accidents, increased sales, reduced turnover, and higher profits and return on investment" (p. 25).

Value. Evaluation is all about "assessing the worth of activities or events according to some system of *valuing*" (Seels and Richey, 1994, p. 52). Value implies that the training program increases the merit or worth of an individual, work group, or organization. The concept of value-added refers to "those activities that provide something the customer values . . . [for example] the difference between the cost of the materials and services purchased to produce a good (or service) and the amount you can sell it for" (Creelman, 2002). Watkins and Kaufman (2002) suggest that both successful needs assessment and evaluation yield internal and external value-added benefits to the organization.

When it comes to evaluation, meaning lies in the eye of the stakeholder. If the stakeholders need to know about the merit or worth of a training program in terms of return on investment, employee satisfaction, or customer loyalty, they are asking about the value of the training program.

Depending on the outcome the stakeholder wishes to achieve, there are several ways to calculate value. For example, there is Gilbert's formula $W = V/C$ (1996, p. 17). In this formula, W stands for worthy performance, V is value (accomplishments), and C is the cost to support the behavior that produces the accomplishment that delivers value to the organization. Worthy performance occurs when the value or accomplishment is greater than the cost of achieving it.

More recently, Van Tiem, Moseley, and Dessinger (2000) set up another equation, $V = f(CC+CE+CQI)$. In this one, ". . . the value of a performance intervention is a function [f] of the continuing competence [CC] of the performers who participate in the intervention, plus the continuing effectiveness [CE] of the entire performance improvement package including products and process, plus the continuing quality improvement [CQI], including quality control and assurance" (p. 176).

Finally, IBM uses Learning Effectiveness Measurement (LEM), a proprietary learning measurement process that constitutes a comprehensive and scaleable framework for deriving higher business value from learning interventions (Spitzer, 2002; Spitzer and Conway, 2002).

Formulate Evaluation Questions. Sometimes it is useful to phrase the stakeholders' information needs as evaluation questions that state or imply the desired evaluation outcome. Combs and Falletta (2000) suggests the use of *targeted* evaluation questions: "Once the intervention [training program] and organizational context are understood, the next step is to generate targeted evaluation questions . . . specific, focused questions that lend themselves to measurement" (p. 18). The stakeholders can help the evaluation, training, or HPT practitioner generate targeted questions. For example, if one intended evaluation outcome is effectiveness, and the goal of the program was to train line operators to know how to assemble a new product, one targeted question might read, "Can training participants assemble the new product within the established standards for number of defects per product run?"

PST 3.5 presents examples of stakeholder need statements, lists and describes confirmative evaluation outcomes, and suggests evaluation questions. The questions are specific to the outcomes and follow the urging of Binder (2001) and other evaluation professionals to state the measure in countable units rather than subjective terms. The practitioner may use a blank version of PST 3.5 to record each stakeholder information need, classify the need according to the four confirmative evaluation outcomes (efficiency, effectiveness, impact, and value), write an evaluation outcome that responds to the need, and write an evaluation question or questions that target the intended outcome.

PST 3.5. From Needs to Outcomes to Questions.

Purpose: To help you record and classify stakeholder needs, write needs-based evaluation outcomes, and write outcome-based evaluation questions.

Directions:

1. Make a blank copy of this matrix and use it as a worksheet.
2. Record a stakeholder information need in Column 1.
3. Classify the need by confirmative evaluation outcome—effectiveness, efficiency, impact, or value—in Column 2.
4. Write the appropriate confirmative evaluation outcome for the need in Column 2.
5. Write a confirmative evaluation question or questions for the outcome in Column 3.
6. Repeat steps 2–5 for each stakeholder need.

1. Stakeholder Information Need	2. Evaluation Outcome	3. Confirmative Evaluation Question
Example: Need to find out whether the training program really did help participants deliver products on time.	**Effectiveness** (degree to which the training program achieved the intended learning or performance goals and objectives)	**Example:** Did distribution areas that participated in the training program increase the number of on-time deliveries by X% per week?
Example: Need to justify the cost of the training program	**Efficiency** (degree to which the benefits of the training outweigh the costs)	**Example:** Do the monetary benefits to the organization outweigh the cost of the training program by X%?
Example: Need to find out whether the training program improved the quality of work output	**Impact** (degree to which the training program outcomes improved the performance of the worker, work, business, or organization)	**Example:** Does the amount of rework show a significant decrease after the training?
Example: Need to find out whether customers think that service is better now	**Value** (degree to which the training program increases the merit or worth of the worker, work, business, or organization)	**Example:** Do annual surveys show X increase in the customer satisfaction index for service calls?

Are Outcomes Evaluable? Now it is time to validate that the stakeholders' information needs have translated successfully into evaluable outcomes. Evaluable outcomes are clear, useful, and measurable. Once again, the evaluator and stakeholder share responsibility for assessing clarity, the stakeholders have the major responsibility for assessing usefulness, and the evaluator has the major responsibility for assessing measurability.

Are Stakeholders Committed to Action? The stakeholders have decided that their information needs and the corresponding evaluation outcomes are evaluable. Now the stakeholders need to commit to personal action for using the outcomes to improve performance. Patton (1997) draws an analogy between utilization-focused evaluation and preparing a meal: ". . . not dining [evaluating] at all is always on the menu. It's better to find out before preparing the meal that those invited to the banquet are not really hungry. Take your feast elsewhere, where it will be savored" (p. 85).

This chapter has suggested a collaborative approach to identifying stakeholder needs and formulating evaluation outcomes. In the spirit of collaboration, stakeholders may find it helpful to share their action plans with each other and even integrate their action plans for maximum effectiveness.

Challenges to Evaluability Assessment

The major challenges facing the evaluation, training, or HPT practitioner during the evaluability assessment stage of planning a confirmative evaluation are to:

- Identify everyone who has a stake in the training program, especially all decision makers
- Include all the stakeholders in the planning activities
- Verify that stakeholder information needs align with the needs of the organization
- Translate stakeholder information needs into confirmative evaluation outcomes that are clear, measurable, and useful
- Maintain support from the stakeholders throughout the confirmative evaluation planning and implementation process

SUMMARY: LESSONS LEARNED IN CHAPTER THREE

1. Reactive planning is real; proactive planning is ideal.

2. The five performance support tools (PSTs) in this chapter can be useful for conducting an evaluability assessment.

3. The keys to successful planning include staying focused on the purpose and context, asking the right people the right questions, negotiating needs and outcomes, and documenting and archiving both the process and the decisions.

4. Personal lessons learned:

NEXT STEPS

Chapter Four discusses how both proactive and reactive planners complete the planning process by developing the confirmative evaluation plan. In addition, proactive planners must monitor the training program for possible revisions and maintain the confirmative evaluation plan until it is implemented.

TOOLBOX FOR ASSESSING EVALUABILITY

Here is your first toolbox. It gives you additional resources to help you increase your knowledge and skills related to evaluability assessment.

Dialogue

Patterson, K., Grenny, J., McMillan, R., and Swizler, A. *Better Than Duct Tape: Dialogue Tools for Getting Results*. Plano, Tex.: Pritchett Rummler-Brache, 2000.

Evaluability Assessment

Smith, M. F. *Evaluability Assessment: A Practical Approach*. Boston: Kluwer, 1989.

Planning Evaluation: Steps and Stages

Shrock, S. A., and Geis, G. L. "Evaluation." In H. D. Stolovitch and E. J. Keeps (eds.), *Handbook of Human Performance Technology: Improving Individual and Organizational Performance Worldwide* (2nd ed.). San Francisco: Jossey-Bass/Pfeiffer; Silver Spring, Md.: International Society for Performance and Instruction, 1999.

Smith, M. E., and Brandenburg, D. C. "Summative Evaluation." *Performance Improvement Quarterly*, 1991, 4(2), 35–58.

Needs Negotiation

Coleman, S. D., Perry, J. D., and Schwen, T. M. "Constructivist Instructional Development: Reflecting on Practice from an Alternative Paradigm." In C. R. Dills and A. J. Romiszowski (eds.), *Instructional Development Paradigms*. Englewood Cliffs, N.J.: Educational Technology Publications, 1997.

Web-Based Resource

The Key Evaluation Checklist, a tool for assessing evaluability, is available at www.wmich.edu/evalctr/checklists

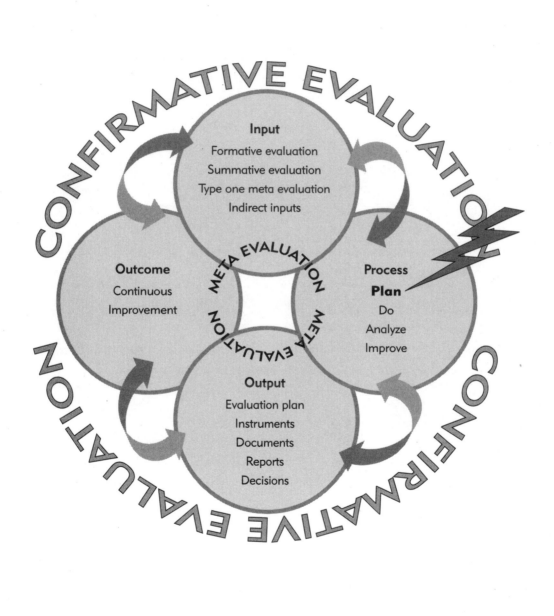

4

Plan: The Plan's the Thing

IN CHAPTER THREE, we began the confirmative evaluation planning process (PST 3.1) by assessing the evaluability of the training program or other performance improvement interventions. Once the training program passes the evaluability assessment, it's time to complete the planning process by developing a plan or blueprint for the confirmative evaluation. A carefully crafted and targeted confirmative evaluation plan accomplishes three things:

1. It sells confirmative evaluation to those people within the organization who will authorize the resources to make it happen (decision makers) or use the results to improve performance.

2. It guides the evaluation, training, or HPT practitioner through the process of implementing confirmative evaluation.

3. It increases the efficiency and effectiveness of the confirmative evaluation process, maximizes the impact and value of the confirmative evaluation results, and limits the need for rework.

Without a systematic and systemic plan, confirmative evaluation would never succeed in accomplishing its goals and would, in fact, justify those who label confirmative evaluation a proverbial exercise in futility.

During this part of the *plan* phase, the practitioner works in partnership with the stakeholders to build a confirmative evaluation plan that ". . . measures the things that are important and to the level of precision that is useful" (Hale, 2002b, n.p.). Building the plan is part salesmanship and part craftsmanship; the decisions made during this phase determine and document who participates in the evaluation, what activities take place, when they take place, how much it costs, what resources are required, how the data are collected and analyzed, and how the results are documented and distributed.

This chapter explains how to build and craft the plan. We focus on the content of the plan and discuss what to include in the executive summary and introduction; how to select and document an evaluation design, a data-collection plan, and a data analysis and interpretation plan; how to develop and document a communication and an administrative plan; and how to gain approval.

After reading this chapter, you will be able to:

1. Explain the purpose of a confirmative evaluation plan

2. Identify the content of a confirmative evaluation plan

3. Use PST 4.1 and PST 4.2 to prepare a complete, accurate, and flexible confirmative evaluation plan

4. Select and document an evaluation design, a data-collection plan, and a data analysis and interpretation plan

5. Develop and document a communication plan

6. Initiate a review-validate-approve cycle for the plan

7. Monitor the training program and maintain the plan (if there is a time lapse between planning and implementing the confirmative evaluation)

What's in a Confirmative Evaluation Plan?

The reactive confirmative evaluation plan is a stand-alone document; the proactive plan is a section within the full-scope evaluation plan for a training program. Whether it is reactive or proactive, the plan must meet the information needs of the people who will authorize the confirmative evaluation, use the results of the confirmative evaluation, and implement the confirmative evaluation. PST 4.1 suggests ways to analyze the target audience, production parameters, and other factors prior to developing the plan.

PST 4.1. Getting Started on a Confirmative Evaluation Plan.

Purpose: To help you plan the plan.

Directions: Fill in the blanks. Add or expand items as needed. For example, complete a stakeholder information section for each person who should review and/or approve the plan.

1. **Training Program:** _____

2. **Type of Plan:** ☐ Proactive plan (section of up-front full-scope evaluation plan)
   ☐ Reactive (stand-alone document)

3. **Stakeholders:** (who should review and/or approve the plan)

Name and Position: _____

Purpose: ☐ Review and approve plan ☐ Review for information only ☐ Not sure

Preferred format: ☐ Hard copy ☐ Electronic copy ☐ Verbal presentation ☐ Other ____

Mail or e-mail address _____

_____

_____

Special information needs _____

_____

Other _____

_____

Name and Position: _____

Purpose: ☐ Review and approve plan ☐ Review for information only ☐ Not sure

Preferred format: ☐ Hard copy ☐ Electronic copy ☐ Verbal presentation ☐ Other ____

Mail or e-mail address _____

_____

_____

Special information needs _____

_____

_____

Other _____

_____

PST 4.1. Getting Started on a Confirmative Evaluation Plan, *Continued*.

Name and Position: _____

Purpose: □ Review and approve plan □ Review for information only □ Not sure

Preferred format: □ Hard copy □ Electronic copy □ Verbal presentation □ Other _____

Mail or e-mail address _____

_____

_____

Special information needs _____

_____

Other _____

_____

4. **Production parameters:** (document standards, technology capabilities, or technology restrictions specific to the organization that may affect how you produce the plan):

    _____

    _____

5. **Outline (PST 4.2):** □ Use "as is" □ Adjust to meet audience needs □ Not sure

Decision makers who will authorize the confirmative evaluation or use the results of the evaluation to improve performance need to know, "What's in it for me and for the organization?" and "How will I know the confirmative evaluation results are valid?" The practitioner and others who will implement the confirmative evaluation must know, "What do I need to do to ensure that the confirmative evaluation is successful?" PST 4.2 lists and describes the content of a confirmative evaluation plan that meets the information needs of decision makers, users, and doers.

PST 4.2. Confirmative Evaluation Plan Outline.

Purpose: To guide the evaluator in preparing a complete and accurate confirmative evaluation plan.

Directions: Use this content outline to develop a confirmative evaluation plan, or as a checklist to verify that the content of the finished plan is complete. Adjust the outline according to the needs of the stakeholders, the reviewers, and the organization (see PST 4.1).

1.0 Executive Summary (single-page summary of plan)

2.0 Introduction (purpose and summary of evaluability assessment)

> 2.1 What is the purpose of this confirmative evaluation?
>
> 2.2 What are the intended evaluation outcomes?
>
> 2.3 Who are the stakeholders?
>
> 2.4 What are the stakeholder information needs?
>
> 2.5 How were the evaluation outcomes formulated?
>
> 2.6 Why is each evaluation outcome important to the stakeholders and the organization?
>
> 2.7 How did we determine that each outcome is evaluable?

3.0 Implementation Plan

> 3.1 Evaluation design
>
>> 3.1.1 Is a formal, informal, or blended evaluation approach most appropriate, given the intended evaluation outcomes and the organizational culture, climate, and capabilities? Why?
>>
>> 3.1.2 Which evaluation design is most appropriate: experimental, quasi-experimental, naturalistic, or blended? Why?
>
> 3.2 Data collection plan
>
>> 3.2.1 What type of data do we need: quantitative, qualitative, or both?
>>
>> 3.2.2 What specific data do we need so as to measure each outcome?

PST 4.2. Confirmative Evaluation Plan Outline, *Continued*.

     3.2.3 What are the data sources?

     3.2.4 What collection techniques are most effective and efficient?

     3.2.5 What data collection tools or instruments do we need to select or design?

     3.2.6 How will we document or record the data?

     3.2.7 How will we store the data for retrieval during analysis and interpretation?

  3.3 Data analysis and interpretation plan

     3.3.1 What techniques will we use to analyze and interpret the data?

     3.3.2 What tools or instruments do we need to select or design?

     3.3.3 Who will do the analysis and interpretation?

  3.4 Communication plan

     3.4.1 Who needs a progress report? Why? How often?

     3.4.2 Who needs to know the results? Why? When?

     3.4.3 How will we communicate the results?

     3.4.4 Who will communicate the results?

     3.4.5 Who will produce the communications?

  3.5 Administration plan

     3.5.1 What administrative activities will support the confirmative evaluation?

     3.5.2 Who will handle the administrative activities?

     3.5.3 What is the budget?

     3.5.4 What are the timelines?

     3.5.5 What are the human resource requirements?

4.0 Conclusion (closing statement)

  4.1 What are the highlights of this plan?

  4.2 Why should the reader buy into this plan?

PST 4.2 suggests that the plan should contain an executive summary, introduction, detailed plan for implementing the confirmative evaluation, and a conclusion to summarize the benefits of the plan and recommend buy-in. The bulk
of the confirmative evaluation plan is really a blueprint for implementing the
evaluation. Although every evaluation is different because of its unique context,
and because procedures differ by method chosen, there are discernible steps that
characterize every well-conducted evaluation. Figure 4.1 lists seven steps for
conducting a successful evaluation (Moseley, 2002). The confirmative evaluation plan should include steps one to six; meta evaluation (step seven) requires
a separate plan or a separate section in the full-scope evaluation plan.

Figure 4.1. Seven Steps to Successful Evaluation.

Step 1 Focus the Evaluation
What   When   Why
Who   Where

Step 2 Design the Evaluation
Data to be collected   Data collection
Methodology   Data analysis
Instrumentation   Reporting

Step 3 Collect the Data
Sources of evaluation information
Quantitative and qualitative data
Select or develop instruments
Questionnaires, interviews, observations, etc.

Step 4 Analyze and Interpret Data
Handling returned data
Analyzing your data
Interpreting results

Step 5 Manage the Evaluation
Select, hire, and train the evaluator
Draft the budget
Monitor the evaluation and anticipate problems

Step 6 Report the Evaluation Results
Identify stakeholders
Online content
Report format

Step 7 Meta Evaluation
Type one or type two?
Who should do it?

Source: Moseley (2002).

Executive Summary

High-level decision makers may never read the entire confirmative evaluation plan. They may prefer a one-page document that states the benefits and contains a synopsis of the major components of the plan. Although the executive summary is first in the outline, it is preferable to write the summary after the entire plan is completed.

Introduction

The introduction sells the confirmative evaluation plan to decision makers and users. The introduction summarizes the process and outcomes of the evaluability assessment (see Chapter Three) and sets forth a strong rationale for spending time, money, and personnel resources on confirmative evaluation. PST 4.2 suggests that the introduction should list and describe the intended confirmative evaluation outcomes, summarize the evaluability assessment process that leads to formulating the outcomes, and stress how the outcomes will trigger and support performance improvement actions that benefit the stakeholders and the organization.

The introduction should specify the purpose of the evaluation and summarize the process and outcomes of the evaluability assessment.

Evaluation Design

The purpose of this section of the confirmative evaluation plan is to:

- Describe the evaluation approach (formal, informal, or blended) and corresponding evaluation design (experimental, quasi-experimental, naturalistic, combination of one or two designs)

- State why the design is appropriate for measuring the intended confirmative evaluation outcomes

- Indicate how the design accommodates the culture and resource capability of the organization

The practitioner who writes this section of the plan needs to know enough about evaluation and the organization to select and justify the most appropriate evaluation approach and design: formal (experimental or quasi-experimental design), informal (naturalistic design), or blended (one or more designs). For example, a knowledgeable evaluator understands that an organization faced with meeting industry performance standards or government certification requirements may be willing to spend time and money for professional evaluators to use an experimental or quasi-experimental design to evaluate their training programs. On the other hand, an organization that is traditionally interested in participant satisfaction is usually more responsive to a naturalistic design such as an immediate reaction survey with follow-up interviews.

Table 4.1 illustrates the three approaches and corresponding confirmative evaluation designs. The left and right columns depict the two extremes of the design continuum, formal and informal. The middle column presents the concept of a blended approach that contains components of formal and informal designs.

Table 4.1. Overview of Evaluation Approaches.

Formal Approach Analyze	Blended Approach Analyze and Ask	Informal Approach "Ask Them"
Experimental design uses random assignment of participants to equalized groups, for example: • True control group (pretest and posttest, or posttest only) • Nonequivalent control group • Single group time series • Time series with nonequivalent group • Before-and-after **Quasi-Experimental design** uses nonrandom assignment to groups, for example: • Interrupted time series • Nonequivalent comparison group • Regression-discontinuity **Quantitative analysis**	**Blended design** combines two or more designs, for example: • True control group and interviews • Single group time series and observation • Nonequivalent comparison group and reaction forms **Quantitative and qualitative analysis**	**Naturalistic design** focuses on the participant, for example: • Open-ended questionnaire or survey • Individual or group interview • Observation • Reaction forms **Qualitative analysis**

The next section of this chapter is an overview of the three evaluation approaches and their corresponding designs.

Formal Approach. The formal approach uses prescribed and systematic evaluation procedures and practices. For example, Carr suggests a process for formal evaluation of training program results that includes these steps:

1. Find at least one measure of current or actual performance.

2. Estimate the performance improvement that should result from the training (ideal).

3. Make improvement expectations clear before and after the training.

4. Measure performance results.

5. Take action. If results meet or exceed performance goals, then maintain training; if results do *not* meet or exceed performance goals, then determine the cause and revise, cancel, or replace training [1992, pp. 149–150].

Boulmetis and Dutwin (2000) stress one limitation to formal evaluation: ". . . formal evaluation will undoubtedly lead to wider disclosure of information to various audiences. When more is known about a program, it is open to more scrutiny and possibly criticism. This is especially threatening to the people involved in the program. . . . They may, therefore, create artificial settings by behaving differently during the evaluation or by providing inaccurate responses in data collection, resulting in a biased evaluation" (pp. 26–27). Specifically, Greenagel (2002) cites three major problems related to formally measuring the effectiveness of e-learning: cost, lack of commitment to measurement, and the fact that "effective e-learning experiences are rarely scalable" (p. 1).

There are two formal designs for evaluation: experimental and quasi-experimental. In experimental designs, participants are randomly assigned to groups; in quasi-experimental designs there is no attempt to achieve random assignment. The use of control groups is prevalent in both experimental and quasi-experimental designs.

Experimental Designs. Experimental designs are inherently formal. The evaluator randomly assigns participants to treatment groups and tries to minimize factors other than treatment that may have an effect on the outcomes. Fitz-Gibbon and Morris (1987, p. 50) list five variations of experimental evaluation design:

1. True control group: pretest-posttest design, or posttest only
2. Nonequivalent control group
3. Single-group time series
4. Time series design with a nonequivalent control group
5. Before-and-after

Designs one, two, and four measure more than one group; they compare the effects of the program with an alternative measurement. Designs three and five measure only the experimental group and are effective for showing how a single program works.

Quasi-Experimental Designs. Quasi-experiments are almost identical to true experiments, except the participants are not randomly assigned to treatment groups. Fitzpatrick, Sanders, and Worthen (2004) and Wholey, Hatry, and Newcomer (1994) describe several types of quasi-experimental design, including interrupted time series, nonequivalent comparison group, and regression-discontinuity. Using any type of quasi-experimental design makes it more difficult to separate the effects of the training program from uncontrollable characteristics of the participants.

Despite this drawback, quasi-experimental designs are useful when random assignment is not feasible—for example, when there is not enough time to randomize participation before the training program begins, the program is already in place and participants were assigned in a nonrandom pattern, participation in a long-term training program has changed over time, or new laws or regulations mandate changes in participation (Wholey, Hatry, and

Newcomer, 1994). Quasi-experimental designs also require the expertise of a professional evaluator as well as organizational support.

Use of Control Groups in Formal Designs. The use of control groups is a component of both experimental and quasi-experimental evaluation designs. Wang (2002) classifies control groups in this way:

- Type one control group: up-front random assignment of participants and double blindness (neither the subject nor the evaluator knows to which group the participant is assigned)

- Type two control group: up-front nonrandom assignment of participants to a group

- Type three control group: up-front assignment of all participants to one group only

- Type four control group: after-the-fact random assignment of participants to a group; relies on participant recall and archived program records (pp. 35–39)

This classification indicates that type one is used in experimental designs while types two through four are used in quasi-experimental designs.

Control Groups in HPT Program Evaluation? Wang (2002) researched the use of control group methods for HPT program evaluation and measurement and suggested that control groups are not generally used in HPT for several reasons:

- HPT professionals lack expertise in statistical analysis.

- Organizations think in terms of *evaluate* rather than *experiment.*

- The intervention plan may not include resources needed for control, such as randomization of participants.

- Evaluation costs money.

- Formal evaluation needs up-front (proactive) planning (pp. 32–42).

Wang (2002, p. 42) concludes: "The fundamental benefit of control group analysis is that it facilitates the evaluation of a given HPT intervention [including a training program] with minimum bias and a known degree of statistical significance."

Informal Approach. An informal approach to confirmative evaluation requires little preliminary planning and results in few planned, long-range consequences. This approach focuses on gathering anecdotal or self-reported information from people and documents. For example, Carr (1992) suggests that training managers who subscribe to MBWA (management by walking around) could ask questions about a training program during their customary stroll through the workplace. The questions should focus on the intended outcome(s) of the confirmative evaluation: effectiveness, efficiency, impact, or value.

Naturalistic Designs. Naturalistic confirmative evaluation designs are informal; they assess the value of a training program without imposing any controls. Many naturalistic evaluation designs tend to be participant-oriented, so this design is also referred to as naturalistic-participant. Actually, naturalistic evaluation focuses on all the stakeholders—their individual values and level of satisfaction with the results of the program (Worthen, Sanders, and Fitzpatrick, 1997). Naturalistic designs are also less dependent on the services of an experienced evaluator, which could lower the cost of the confirmative evaluation.

Along the same lines, Bergman and Jacobson (2000) state that "Your organization's single most important *business result* is customer satisfaction"(p. 69). We suggest that the best way to measure the business results of a training program and gauge training's real impact is to ask internal and external customers *targeted questions* about the training program. We also feel that asking the customers makes the customers happy, demonstrates to employees that the organization is truly committed to customer satisfaction, and tells trainers that their value is based on "the extent that employees do things differently after the training" (p. 72).

Blended Designs. Shrock and Geis (1999) picture evaluation methodology as a continuum. At one end, experimental evaluation methodology relies on the statistical analysis of randomly selected control groups versus treatment groups, taking into account the variables that could affect the outcomes. Both input and output data are generally objective and quantitative, so they are expressed in numbers. At the other end of the continuum, naturalistic evaluation may include an analysis of existing documentation or strategies such as interviews, observations, focus groups, and surveys. The evaluator assumes that not all outcomes are predictable up front; important outcomes may surface during evaluation. Input and output data are usually subjective or qualitative, so they are expressed primarily in words and focus on trends or patterns.

Evaluation methodology that blends quantitative and qualitative elements—for example, surveys that ask both open-ended and closed questions—fall between the two ends of the continuum. Blended designs may contain elements of formal and informal evaluation. For example, an evaluator may suggest measuring cost and test results (quantitative), collecting participant reactions (qualitative), using random assignment (experimental), and collecting data from focus groups (naturalistic) to judge the efficiency or effectiveness of a training program compared to other training programs or delivery systems.

Data-Collection Plan. The data-collection plan for a confirmative evaluation should include this information:

- What data are needed to measure the intended long-term outcomes of the training program, given the selected evaluation design?
- What are the sources for the data?
- Who will collect the data?
- What techniques and tools are most useful for collecting, documenting, storing, and retrieving the data?

The responses to these questions vary with the nature and complexity of the organization and the training program, stakeholder information needs, intended long-term evaluation outcomes, the requirements of the evaluation design, and the organization's computer and telecommunications capabilities.

Types of Data. Different confirmative evaluation outcomes are measured using different data. For example, Jackson (1989) suggests that if the intended outcome is to measure training program effectiveness, then the practitioner may want to collect before-and-after data on desired performance (objectives) and actual performance (results) at two levels, corporate and operational. Spitzer (2002, p. 2) suggests that if the intended outcome is "measuring the bottom-line business value of training, both quantitatively and qualitatively," then the evaluation, training, or HPT professional may collect up-front and results-based data from "five interrelated analyses: organizational, performance, causal chain, training benefit/cost, and training investment analysis."

The data-collection section plan should specify whether the practitioner needs quantitative data, qualitative data, or both to measure the intended confirmative evaluation outcomes. Quantitative data are expressed in numbers, may be analyzed using statistical tests, and result in an objective description of what is being evaluated. Qualitative data are expressed in words, require an inductive approach to data analysis, and result in a subjective description of what is being evaluated. Table 4.2 lists examples of quantitative and qualitative data that are useful for measuring training program efficiency, effectiveness, impact, and value.

Table 4.2. Types of Data for Judging Confirmative Evaluation Outcomes.

To Measure	Collect These Data:
Effectiveness	**Quantitative (measurable)** • Pretest and posttest results from training program • Workplace data (statistics and counts related to pretraining and posttraining production, sales, accidents, attendance, cycle time, rework, and so forth) • Frequency data • Quantifiable cost-benefit data • Other effectiveness-related quantitative data

Table 4.2. Types of Data for Judging Confirmative Evaluation Outcomes, *Continued*.

To Measure	Collect These Data:
Effectiveness	**Qualitative (subjective)** • Reaction of participant, supervisor, or customer to training program • Self-reported transfer of training • Employee morale • Customer satisfaction • Other effectiveness-related qualitative data
Efficiency	**Quantitative** • Cost of designing, developing, implementing, and evaluating training program • Cost per participant to attend training • Costs of alternate delivery systems • Quantifiable benefit data • Frequency data • Pre-and-post costs for rework, insurance, lost production time • Other efficiency-related quantitative data **Qualitative** • Nonquantifiable benefit data (customer satisfaction, employee satisfaction) • Expert review • Other efficiency-related qualitative data
Impact	**Quantitative** • Changes in market share • Cost data • Quantifiable benefit data

Table 4.2. Types of Data for Judging Confirmative Evaluation Outcomes, *Continued*.

To Measure	Collect These Data:
	• Changes in trends • Global business measures • Frequency data • Other impact-related quantitative data **Qualitative** • Nonquantifiable benefit data (perceptions of benefit from such stakeholders as participants, managers, customers, experts, and others) • Other impact-related qualitative data
Value	**Quantitative** • Time series data • Regression data • Return-on-investment data • Economic indicators • Econometric models • Other value-related quantitative data **Qualitative** • Executive opinions • Customer market data • Salesforce composite data • Delphi data • Other value-related qualitative data

Binder (2002c, n.p.) offers a rule of thumb to help the practitioner decide whether to select quantitative or qualitative data: ". . . when we decide to measure the results of our interventions on behavior, job outputs, or business results, we should start with measures of countable, standard units and not stray very far from those measures. If we report and rely primarily on percentage scores, rather than on the measures themselves, we're as likely as not to introduce misunderstandings and misguided decisions without even knowing it."

Organizational culture and political realities may also help determine which type of data is most appropriate. For example:

- Will a specific work group agree to share data that compare product quality before and after training?

- Will individual performers or unions view the collection of performance analysis data as a backdoor attempt to use the information for salary or promotion purposes?

Data Sources. The confirmative evaluation plan should also list and describe the sources for the confirmative evaluation data. Brinkerhoff, Brethower, Hluchyj, and Nowakowski (1983) discuss four general sources of evaluation data: people, documentation, context, and performance. People sources may include all clients, audiences, subjects, experts who share specific knowledge or expertise, and stakeholders for whom the evaluation has meaning or significance (for example, decision makers or those who are affected positively or negatively through practices, processes, or values). Documentation is an endless source and may include organizationwide or business group documents, on-the-shelf reports, fiscal records, expenditure reports, meeting minutes, interim and occasional reports, and announcements. Context is a broad source of data, which may include the facilities in which the evaluation occurred, leadership and management styles of key personnel, political forces, economic realities, institutional and product-specific trends, or organizational culture. Performance sources could be people, documentation, or context (for example, on-the-job observations; interviews with performers, supervisors, and customers; work samples; expert review; performance intervention documentation; ergonomic or other studies of the work environment; performance standards; test scores; and a variety of job-specific measures).

Gibson, Ivancevich, and Donnelly (1997) also suggest that the outcomes of individual performance constitute a rich data source for evaluating training program effectiveness, efficiency, and impact: "The first-level outcomes resulting from behavior are associated with doing the job itself. These outcomes include productivity, absenteeism, turnover, and quality of productivity. Second-level outcomes are those events (rewards or punishments) that the first-level outcomes are likely to produce, such as merit pay increase, group acceptance or rejection, and promotion" (p. 158).

Examples of Potential Performance Data and Sources. One way to begin identifying what to measure is to review existing documentation to discover the organization's "current strategic measures." For example:

- Business result: bottom-line financial and nonfinancial measures
- Organizational effectiveness: measures used for monitoring and managing the organization as a whole
- Functional or process: measures used to monitor and manage functions or processes within an organization
- Human performance: measures of individual and team performance (Spitzer and Conway, 2002, p. 5)

If documentation is not available, Spitzer and Conway suggest, the information may be available from financial or business analysts, functional leaders, or process owners.

Data Collectors. The confirmative evaluation plan should include a list, or at least a general description, of who will collect the evaluation data. The evaluation, training, and HPT practitioner may collect the data for small-scale confirmative evaluations. Large-scale confirmative evaluation efforts that last three to six months or longer may require the services of a project manager and an evaluation team. The confirmative evaluation team may consist of program managers, division staff, regional office staff, training department staff, statisticians, design specialists, instructors, field employees, trained volunteers, and others whose specialized knowledge and skills, or access to the required data, will aid the collection process.

Data-Collection Techniques, Tools, Technology. The confirmative evaluation plan should include a list and brief description of the data-collection techniques, tools, and technology. Data collection should also include plans for collecting, recording, and storing quantitative and quantitative data. The practitioner should select the most appropriate technique(s) depending on the type of data required (quantitative or qualitative), the source of the data (people, documentation, context, or performance), and the culture and capability of the organization.

Table 4.3 lists the major data-collection techniques (interview, group activity, observation, survey, self-report, review of existing documents) and suggests some tools and technology to support each technique. All the techniques are suitable, whether the source is people, context, or performance; when the source is documentation, document review is most appropriate. An experienced evaluator can adapt most data-collection tools to collect quantitative or qualitative data.

Table 4.3. Data-Collection Techniques, Tools, and Technology.

Technique	Tools	Technology
Interview • Structured • Unstructured	• Script with space to record responses (print or electronic) • Audiotape, recorder, player, transcription device • Video camera, tape, player • Camcorder, tape • Printout of online interview • Database and spreadsheet software	• Face-to-face • Telephone • Online chat room or instant message • Online meeting with audio/video • Satellite broadcast with one-way or two-way audio/video

Table 4.3. Data-Collection Techniques, Tools, and Technology, *Continued*.

Technique	Tools	Technology
Group Activity • Brainstorming • Consensus • Critical incident • Focus group • Nominal group • Storytelling	• Activity guide • Template to record responses • Database and spreadsheet software • Audiotape, recorder, player, transcription device • Video camera, tape, player • Camcorder, tape • Meeting software or third-party provider • Printout of online activities	• Face-to-face • Electronic whiteboards • Telephone conferencing (licensed access or third-party provider) • Online chat room • Online meeting with audio/video • Keypad response system • Satellite broadcast with one-way or two-way audio/video • Electronic bulletin boards
Survey	• Survey or questionnaire (electronic or print-based form) • Database and spreadsheet software • Template to summarize responses (electronic or print-based) • Survey software or third-party service provider • Printout of online activity	• Face-to-face • Fax • Snail mail • E-mail • Telephone • Online chat room or instant message • Keypad response system
Observation	• Observation guide or checklist with space to record comments (electronic or print-based) • Template to summarize observation (electronic or print-based) • Database and spreadsheet software • Audiotape, recorder, player, transcription device • Video camera, tape, player • Camcorder, tape	• Real-time • Video • Satellite broadcast • Telephone (telephone sales skills, hotline response, etc.)

Table 4.3. Data-Collection Techniques, Tools, and Technology, *Continued*.

Technique	Tools	Technology
Self-reporting	• Diary, journal, or log (electronic or print-based) • Case studies, scenarios, and stories • Templates for all of the above and to summarize responses (electronic or print-based)	• Real-time • E-mail • Electronic bulletin boards
Document review	• Storage for print-based documents • Scanning technology • Storage for online documents • Database and spreadsheet software • Case studies and scenarios • Online search engines	• Print-based libraries or document depositories • Internet or intranet sites • Information or knowledge management systems

Data Analysis and Interpretation Plan

It is also important to select data analysis and interpretation techniques up front and describe them in the confirmative evaluation plan. Selecting the appropriate data analysis and interpretation techniques depends on the evaluation design, the qualifications of the person doing the analysis and interpretation, and the intended confirmative evaluation outcome.

The evaluator who selects an experimental or quasi-experimental confirmative evaluation design will also select an appropriate statistical test to analyze the data—for example, measures of central tendencies (mean, median, mode), or measures of dispersion (standard deviation, t test, and so forth). The evaluator who selects a naturalistic confirmative evaluation design may use frequency counts; describe the documentation or the responses; or divide and classify the responses into themes, types, trends, or time periods.

The quality of analysis and interpretation depends on the *goodness* of the data, the experience and skill of the evaluator, and the capability of the organization. Statistical analysis and the interpretation of statistical results are skills that require specialized education or training (for example, university courses in statistics or "Black Belt" training in organizations with Six Sigma quality initiatives). Organizations with access to professional internal or external evaluators and computer-based statistical analysis programs are best able to analyze and interpret formal, experimental confirmative evaluation designs.

Data analysis and interpretation techniques are also based on intended confirmative evaluation outcomes. The analyst may compare delivery systems to determine effectiveness or efficiency; compare costs and benefits to determine effectiveness, efficiency, or impact; perform an impact assessment (impact); or compute return on investment to determine value. In all cases, it is vital that analysts communicate both the positive and negative; decision makers need to realize what they stand to gain and what they may have to relinquish to obtain it (Worthen and Sanders, 1987).

Comparison Analysis. One way to evaluate effectiveness or efficiency is to compare program methodology or delivery systems. To analyze data related to methods, media, or delivery systems, the practitioner must know the criteria for evaluating the learning and instruction technologies involved in the comparison study.

The criteria should be established during the formative or summative evaluation planning stage, and the results should be available to the confirmative evaluator. Otherwise, it falls to the practitioner to set evaluation criteria for comparing the instructional or learning technologies. Shank (2001) offers a rule of thumb for evaluating e-learning that the practitioner may apply to all learning delivery technologies: "learning is learning is learning . . . and everything you know about good learning applies to e-learning" (n.p.). Sanders (1999) suggests ". . . the evaluator must assess how well the technology performed: Did the learners enjoy using the technology? Were they able to learn from it? Did the technology perform up to expectations?" (p. 36).

Some criteria are intrinsic to specific instructional media and technology. Distance learning technology may include visual, auditory, and text components, and each of these components has a specific set of criteria to determine effectiveness in a learning context. The challenge lies in the need to "strike a balance [between] technological issues and humanistic issues . . ." (Sanders, 1999, p. 36).

Comparison analysis is also useful for determining the impact of a training program: "The basic aim of an impact assessment is to produce an estimate of the net effects of an intervention—that is, an estimate of the impact of the intervention uncontaminated by the influence of other processes and events that also may affect the behavior or conditions" (Rossi, Freeman, and Lipsey, 1999, p. 235). During impact assessment, the evaluator estimates the difference between what would happen if a training program is implemented and what would happen if it is not implemented. An appropriate, well-designed assessment "isolates the effects of extraneous factors so that observed differences can safely be attributed to the intervention" (Rossi, Freeman, and Lipsey, 1999, p. 258).

Cost Analysis. Cost analysis is another way to analyze efficiency, effectiveness, impact, and value. According to Rossi, Freeman, and Lipsey (1999), "Knowledge of the extent to which programs have been implemented successfully and the degree to which they have produced the desired outcomes is indispensable to program managers, stakeholders, and policy makers. In almost all cases, however, it is just as critical to be informed about how program outcomes compare to their costs" (p. 365).

Discussions by Levin (1983) and Worthen and Sanders (1987) help the practitioner select which type of cost analysis is most appropriate for evaluating the intended outcomes of a training program. In each type of cost-benefit analysis (CBA), monetary or other quantitative values are assigned to both sides of the equation:

- Cost-benefit analysis compares the costs and benefits of a single program or alternative programs; the goal is to justify the costs of a single program or identify which program yields the highest benefits for the lowest cost.
- Cost-effectiveness analysis compares the costs of alternative programs to assess the degree to which the programs meet or exceed their goals and objectives (effectiveness); the goal is to select the program that costs the least to achieve the highest level of effectiveness.

- Cost-utility analysis compares the cost and estimated usefulness of alternative programs; the goal is to select the program with the lowest cost and highest estimated positive impact on performance improvement.
- Cost-feasibility analysis compares the cost of each program with the available budget; the goal is to make decisions on the basis of available resources.

Sometimes it is difficult to verify that a training program really caused improved performance or other desired outcome. Dixon (1990) describes a causal model of cost analysis, which is useful when impact is the intended confirmative evaluation outcome. Dixon's causal model "builds a chain of logic that increases the likelihood of determining if the increase can be attributed to the change in behavior" (pp. 157–158).

Return on Investment (ROI) Analysis. The times they are a-changing. Knowledge and skill were (and still may be) considered intangible assets that are not recorded on a balance sheet. However, "the telecommunications and systems infra-structure necessary to deliver e-learning does appear on the balance sheet, so ROI has become a tool of the trade in training departments" (Greenagel, 2002, p. 2). Today, evaluation, training, and HPT practitioners might select ROI analysis as the tool of choice to evaluate the impact and value of a training program, especially if they can make a case for a one-to-one relationship between change in behavior and business indicators (Dixon, 1990).

For example, Nextel's HRD organization developed and uses *The Training Scorecard* to confirm the ROI of selected training programs. *Scorecard* is based on Jack Phillips's ROI Process and Donald Kirkpatrick's four levels of evaluation: "*The Training Scorecard* . . . ensures that the HRD organization is focused on delivering training focused on business needs. It also provides a way to easily communicate training results to the client groups, including executives" (Schmidt, 2002, n.p.).

Watkins and Kaufman (2002) suggest that "when making decisions, managers are often initially interested in data reflecting the organization's performance status on two points: intended results (Point A) and obtained results (Point B)" (p. 24). Watkins and Kaufman feel there is a whole area of concern between these two points that may be categorized as ROI with a twist of "what would have been," or cost-consequence analysis (CCA):

- "What is the cost of going from intended to obtained results?

- What is the value of obtained results in relation to intended results?

- What would have been the cost of using an alternative intervention to go from obtained to required results?

- What would have been the consequence of not going from obtained to required results?

- What is the value of required results in relation to obtained results?" (pp. 24–25)

Communication Plan

The communication section of the confirmative evaluation plan should include certain information:

- Person responsible for implementing the communication plan: evaluation, training, or HPT practitioner, confirmative evaluation project manager

- Audience: all stakeholders, especially those who are responsible for the confirmative evaluation (owners), support it, need to approve activities or documents, or have to be kept informed

- Purpose: inform, seek approval, report findings, and so forth

- Type: formal or informal memo, meeting, e-mail, presentation to management, report, and so forth

- Schedule: as needed or requested, based on specific trigger events (instruments ready for approval, data analysis completed, and so forth)

- Special production requirements: word processing, graphics, interface with existing information or knowledge management system, and so forth

Administration Plan

Managing a confirmative evaluation is very much like managing any other project. The administration plan includes:

- Name or job description of the person responsible for managing the confirmative evaluation or performing the administrative activities (the practitioner, the project manager, an administrative assistant)

- List of all management and administrative activities and tasks required to support the confirmative evaluation plan

- Timeline with start and end dates for each activity and task

- Budget for planning, implementing, and evaluating (meta) the confirmative evaluation

Project management software is useful for planning, recording, and reporting progress. The software can generate reports: activity or task lists, resource allocation, start and end dates, PERT and Gantt charts, budgets, and others that may be downloaded directly into the administration plan.

Review, Validate, and Approve the Plan

The final step in developing the confirmative evaluation plan is to review, validate, and approve the plan. First, the practitioner reviews the evaluability assessment process to make certain the process was sound and the results are valid. He or she may also ask one or more informed colleagues or an independent evaluator to review and validate the evaluability assessment.

The next step is to ask the stakeholders to verify that the confirmative evaluation plan is clear, unambiguous, and complete and that it accurately reflects the needs of all the stakeholders. The evaluation, training, or HPT practitioner may also ask colleagues or an independent evaluator to evaluate the plan according to standard evaluation practices.

The final step is to present the plan to management, either as part of the full-scope evaluation plan (proactive) or as a stand-alone plan (reactive), and seek approval to implement the reactive plan or maintain the proactive plan until it is time to implement the confirmative evaluation. After the reactive or proactive plan is reviewed, approved, and validated, the practitioner should document the process for developing the plan and archive the process documents along with the completed confirmative evaluation plan.

SUMMARY: LESSONS LEARNED IN CHAPTER FOUR

1. It's important to have a plan, whether it is proactive or reactive.

2. The success of a confirmative evaluation is largely dependent on the technical expertise of an evaluator working within a supportive and professional business milieu.

3. A variety of quantitative and qualitative data are used to measure effectiveness, efficiency, impact, and value.

4. Personal lessons learned:

   _____

   _____

   _____

   _____

   _____

   _____

   _____

   _____

NEXT STEPS

The next chapter discusses *do*: how to maintain a proactive confirmative evaluation plan prior to implementation and how to implement a proactive or reactive plan, including how to select or develop data-collection tools and instruments and collect the data.

TOOLBOX FOR PREPARING A CONFIRMATIVE EVALUATION PLAN

Preparing the confirmative evaluation plan requires general knowledge and skills related to project management, evaluation (including how to evaluate various learning and instruction technologies), and analysis. In addition to a comprehensive book on statistical analysis, a statistical analysis software package (such as SPSS/SPSSX; www.spss.com), and a project management software package (such as Microsoft Project), the professional resources listed here provide help in planning confirmative evaluation and preparing a successful plan.

Cost-Benefit Analysis (CBA)

Hartley, D. E. "E-Valuation: Pricing E-learning." *Training and Development,* 2001, 55(4), 24–28.

Kearsley, G. "Analyzing the Cost and Benefits of Training: Part 1—An Introduction." *Performance and Instruction Journal,* Feb. 1986, 25(1), 30–32.

Kearsley, G. "Analyzing the Cost and Benefits of Training: Part 2—Identifying the Costs and Benefits." *Performance and Instruction Journal,* Apr. 1986, 25(3), 23–25.

Kearsley, G. "Analyzing the Cost and Benefits of Training: Part 3—Formulating Models." *Performance and Instruction Journal,* May 1986, 25(4), 13–15.

Kearsley, G. "Analyzing the Cost and Benefits of Training: Part 4—Data Collection." *Performance and Instruction Journal,* June–July 1986, 25(5), 8–10.

Kearsley, G. "Analyzing the Cost and Benefits of Training: Part 5—Putting the Results into Action." *Performance and Instruction Journal,* Aug. 1986, 25(6), 8–10.

Cost Feasibility and Utility Analysis

Wholey, J. S. "Assessing the Feasibility and Likely Usefulness of Evaluation," In J. S. Wholey, H. P. Hatry, and K. E. Newcomer (eds.), *Handbook of Practical Program Evaluation*. San Francisco: Jossey-Bass, 1994.

Evaluating Instructional and Learning Technologies

Bersin, J. "Measure the Metrics." *e-learning,* June 2002, 3(6), 26–28.

Heinich, R., Molenda, M., Russell, J. D., and Smaldino, S. E. *Instructional Media and Technologies for Learning* (5th ed.). Upper Saddle River, N.J.: Prentice Hall, 1996.

TOOLBOX FOR PREPARING A CONFIRMATIVE EVALUATION PLAN, *Continued*

Evaluation

Fitzpatrick, J. L., Sanders, J. R., and Worthen, B. R. *Program Evaluation: Alternative Approaches and Practical Guidelines* (3rd ed.). Boston: Pearson/Allyn and Bacon, 2004.

Hale, J. *Performance-Based Evaluation: Tools and Techniques to Measure the Impact of Training.* San Francisco: Jossey-Bass/Pfeiffer, 2002.

Rossi, P. H., Freeman, H. E., and Lipsey, M. W. *Evaluation: A Systematic Approach* (6th ed.). Thousand Oaks, Calif.: Sage, 1999.

Worthen, B. R., Sanders, J. R., and Fitzpatrick, J. L. *Program Evaluation: Alternative Approaches and Practical Guidelines* (2nd ed.). White Plains, N.Y.: Longman, 1997.

Project Management

Fuller, J. *Managing Performance Improvement Projects: Preparing, Planning, Implementing.* San Francisco: Jossey-Bass/Pfeiffer, with International Society for Performance Improvement (ISPI), 1997.

Greer, M. *ID Project Management: Tools and Techniques for Instructional Designers and Developers.* Englewood Cliffs, N.J.: Educational Technology Publications, 1992.

Greer, M. *The Project Manager's Partner: A Step-by-Step Guide to Project Management.* Amherst, Mass.: HRD Press, 1996.

Phillips, J. J., Bothell, T. W., and Snead, G. L. *The Project Management Scorecard: Measuring the Success of Project Management Solutions.* Boston: Butterworth, Heinemann/Elsevier Science, 2002.

Return on Investment (ROI) Analysis

Phillips, J. J. (ed.). *In Action: Measuring Return on Investment: Eighteen Case Studies from the Real World of Training, Vol 1.* Alexandria, Va: American Society for Training & Development, 1994.

Phillips, J. J. *Return on Investment in Training and Performance Improvement Programs* (2nd ed.). St. Louis, Mo: Elsevier, 2003.

Phillips, J., Pulliam, P. F., and Wurtz, W. Level 5 Evaluation: ROI. (*Info-line*, no. 9805). Alexandria, Va.: American Society for Training and Development, May 1998.

TOOLBOX FOR PREPARING A CONFIRMATIVE EVALUATION PLAN, *Continued*

Web-Based Resource

Refereed checklists and other resources for designing, budgeting, contracting, staffing, managing program evaluation are available at www.wmich.edu/evalctr/checklists

See also www.ASTD.org for information on the organization's special interest group of members who discuss and use ROI.

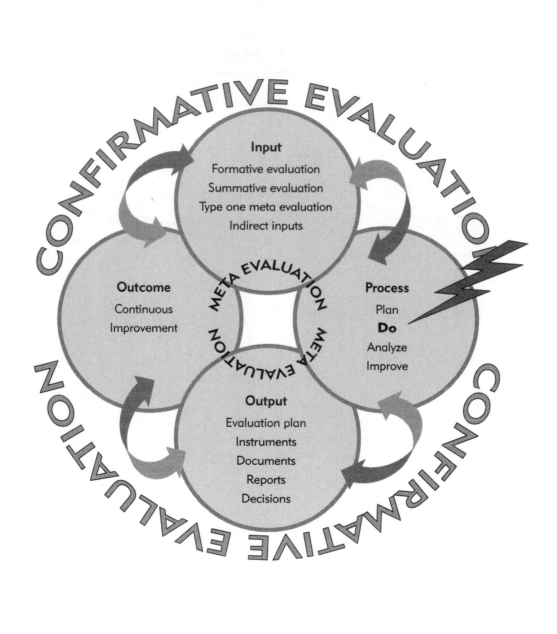

5

Do: For Goodness' Sake

THE MILITARY and other organizations sometimes use the term *goodness* to qualify the degree to which people, places, situations, or things meet stated or implicit standards for excellence and integrity. The maxim is *goodness follows goodness*. If a training program is good in terms of the ISD standards for design and delivery, it will meet the stated goals and objectives. In the case of confirmative evaluation, the goodness trail begins with the evaluability assessment of the training program (Chapter Three), which looks at intended program duration, organization-specific criteria, stakeholder information needs, and intended evaluation outcomes. The goodness of the evaluability assessment directly affects the goodness of the confirmative evaluation plan (Chapter Four), and the goodness of the plan directly affects the goodness of the data-collection process, which is the main activity of the *do* phase and the topic for this chapter.

This chapter begins with a discussion of why, when, and how to verify the goodness of a *proactive* plan before collecting the data. (We assume the goodness of a *reactive* evaluability assessment and confirmative evaluation plan, since both were conducted just prior to beginning data collection.) The rest of the chapter focuses on how to select or develop the data-collection instruments, train the data collectors if necessary, collect and store the data, and document and archive the data-collection process. We weave challenges and examples throughout the chapter and present a Toolbox of resources for selecting or developing data-collection tools. We encourage the evaluation, training, or HPT practitioner to stay focused on the confirmative evaluation plan, especially the intended evaluation outcomes, the targeted evaluation questions, and the selected evaluation design.

We also try to indicate who will perform or be responsible for the various activities that make up the *do* phase of the confirmative evaluation process. The primary responsibility for the success of the data-collection activities is shared by the people who handle the data—the practitioner and project manager planning and managing the activities; the data collector who gathers the information required to measure the intended evaluation outcomes; and the people who provide the data. In a small organization, the practitioner may also take the role of data collector, project manager, and even analyst, so roles and responsibilities will overlap. In large organizations, the evaluation, training, or HPT practitioner may train one or more data collectors, and a project manager will administer the resources and activities.

After reading this chapter, you will be able to:

1. Explain how reactive and proactive planning affects the start-up strategy for data collection

2. Describe the process for collecting data for confirmative evaluation

3. Identify the challenges to data collection

4. Take action to ensure that data collection follows professional, quality standards for program evaluation

Jump-Start Data Collection

Chapter Two discussed the benefits and drawbacks of reactive and proactive planning. The practitioner may begin the official confirmative evaluation process as soon as the reactive confirmative evaluation plan is approved; this is one benefit of just-in-time planning. The practitioner does not begin the official confirmative evaluation for three to twelve months or more after the proactive plan is approved; this is one potential drawback of up-front planning. During the gap between planning and implementation, elements of the plan can and probably will change:

- Intended evaluation outcomes, scope, or purpose: changes in other elements may trigger a change in the original rationale for planning the confirmative evaluation

- Stakeholder information needs: changes in the workplace may make it necessary to add or delete specific needs

- Resources: the allocation or availability of budget, data, facilities, materials, people, time, or required hard and soft technology may change

- Data-collection methodology: ethical, legal, or political issues may require changes in the original data-collection plan

- Organizational or stakeholder commitment: changes in global or organizational climate or culture, or in personnel, may alter the level of commitment to confirmative evaluation

- Training program: revisions as a result of formative or summative evaluation activities may require a change in the confirmative evaluation design

A change in even one element may challenge the evaluation, training, or HPT practitioner to think outside the box, be flexible, be creative, and be ready to identify and suggest change-based actions.

The practitioner, perhaps with assistance from the data collector or analyst, has two basic options for dealing with change: (1) continuously or periodically monitor the training program, maintain the confirmative evaluation plan, revise the plan as needed, and communicate with the stakeholders until it is time to officially start confirmative evaluation; or (2) review the original plan and communicate with the stakeholders as a one-time-only activity, just before it is time to begin confirmative evaluation.

The goal of both options is to verify that the training program, stakeholder information needs, and intended evaluation outcomes are still current and evaluable. This is especially crucial when the organization needs the information from the evaluation for certification, licensing, quality, legal, or other requirements. The benefit of the first option is that it jump-starts the confirmative evaluation *do* phase and strengthens the concept of seamless, integrated, full-scope evaluation.

When a change is identified, the practitioner may suggest several action options:

- Revise the confirmative evaluation plan to adjust to organizational changes
- Adapt the data-collection or analysis strategy to accommodate changes in technology
- Add or delete stakeholders or information resources
- Cancel the confirmative evaluation

Maintain the Plan

Once the full-scope evaluation plan is reviewed, approved, and validated, the practitioner may decide to maintain the plan until it is time to conduct confirmative evaluation. Maintaining the plan takes advantage of the two major benefits of proactive planning: (1) all types of training program evaluation are integrated, so the outputs and outcomes of each type should support each other's needs; and (2) ongoing maintenance of the confirmative evaluation plan may be planned and scheduled up front in the original full-scope plan. The most effective way to maintain the plan is to monitor the training program, especially the formative and summative evaluation outputs and outcomes, and make revisions to the plan as needed—or at least set up yellow warning flags that change may have an impact on the plan.

The evaluation, training, or HPT practitioner, analyst, or data collector monitors the training program by collecting and analyzing data from formative and summative evaluation, staying abreast of training program and organizational changes, and documenting whether evaluation outcomes or program changes require modifications to the confirmative evaluation plan. Monitoring the training program saves time in this phase of the confirmative evaluation process and helps ensure that data are not lost.

If the organization has a knowledge or information management system in place, the practitioner should have access to all the tools and techniques that are required to retrieve, document, and archive feedback from the training program and the organization. Otherwise, he or she may need to work with whatever system is used by the training and development or HRD group within the organization.

The practitioner then analyzes the data from monitoring activities and reviews and revises the plan when changes in stakeholders, stakeholder needs, evaluation outcomes, the training program, or the organization trigger the need for change. The stakeholders must review and approve all changes prior to implementation of the confirmative evaluation. The practitioner may set up a schedule of revision cycles based on the time gap between planning and implementation (a three-month gap may only require one revision cycle, while a one-year gap requires two or three revision cycles).

Just-in-Time Review

If resources or commitment issues do not support ongoing maintenance of the confirmative evaluation plan, the practitioner may conduct a last-minute reality check as the time approaches to implement the confirmative evaluation. Again, the goal is to make sure that the training program is still evaluable and that stakeholder information needs and intended evaluation outcomes are still current and evaluable. The practitioner reviews formative and summative evaluation outcomes and changes to the organization, training program, stakeholders, stakeholder needs, or intended evaluation outcomes to determine whether there is a need to make changes to the proactive confirmative evaluation plan. If it is necessary to revise the plan, the practitioner should make sure the stakeholders review and approve any changes prior to implementation.

Focus Data Collection

The practitioner has the main responsibility for making sure everyone who is involved in the confirmative evaluation stays focused on the evaluation plan, especially the intended evaluation outcomes and the data-collection design and strategy. One way to stay focused is to use a matrix summarizing and linking each intended evaluation outcome with the required data, potential data sources, and strategies for retrieving and storing the data for future analysis. PST 5.1 helps the data collector stay focused on the intended evaluation outcome and evaluation question and is also helpful for communicating with the stakeholders.

PST 5.1. Matrix to Focus and Plan Data Collection.

Purpose: To help the data collector focus on each evaluation outcome and question and document a data-collection plan.

Directions:

1. Review the sample matrix.

2. Prepare one matrix for each intended confirmative evaluation outcome and the related evaluation question(s). Note that it is possible to have more than one evaluation question for an outcome. If so, complete a separate matrix for each evaluation question.

3. Complete the matrix for the first confirmative evaluation outcome and evaluation question.

   Column 1: Record your first data source and where to find it.

   Column 2: List the collection techniques and tools you will use to gather the data from this source.

   Column 3: Record how and where you will store the data you have collected.

4. Repeat step three until all possible data sources, collection techniques and tools, and storage requirements are documented for the evaluation question.

5. Go on to the matrix for the next evaluation question or the next outcome.

6. If the matrices are completed during proactive planning, review and revise as needed before you begin the confirmative evaluation.

PST 5.1. Matrix to Focus and Plan Data Collection, *Continued*.

Sample Matrix

Training program: New Product Update		
Intended evaluation outcome: Judge the effectiveness of new product training program for sales representatives		
Evaluation question: Did customer satisfaction with the product knowledge of sales representatives increase by X percent after training?		
Type of data: Quantitative and qualitative data on customer perception of sales representative product knowledge before and after training		
Data collector: Mark Smith		
Date: December 2003–December 2004		

Where will we find the data?	How will we collect the data (techniques and tools)?	How will we store the data?
Customer satisfaction surveys (before and after training) • Marketing department • Information system	Extant data analysis • Matrix • Online database to record data • Evaluation project online folder • Scanner	Store responses so they may be sorted and analyzed by: • Product • Date (before and after training) • Instructional strategy • Rating scale responses Archive original surveys or tabulations in evaluation project online folder
Customers who interfaced with sales representatives before and after training • Random selection • 10% of total population	Focus groups • Script • Electronic whiteboard • Participant handout with instructions	Record responses on electronic whiteboard and store in evaluation project online folder Sort and tabulate responses by: • Product • Date (before and after training) • Instructional strategy Archive videotape of focus group in evaluation project online folder

PST 5.1. Matrix to Focus and Plan Data Collection, *Continued*.

Blank Matrix

Training program:

Intended evaluation outcome:

Evaluation question:

Type of data:

Data collector:

Date:

Where will we find the data?	How will we collect the data (techniques and tools)?	How will we store the data?

The practitioner may develop the matrix in the *plan* phase and include it in the confirmative evaluation plan, or develop the matrix with the data collector as part of a focusing activity. A just-in-time focusing activity has the advantage of turning PST 5.1 into an advanced organizer for the practitioner as well as the data collectors.

Collect the Data

The confirmative evaluation plan should identify the techniques and tools for collecting the data. The term *technique* refers to the method(s) the data collector uses to gather data; the term *tool* refers to the guides and other instruments the data collector uses to perform the technique. There are five basic techniques for collecting confirmative evaluation data (extant data analysis, group activities, interviews, observation, and surveys), all of which are discussed later in this chapter. They are the same techniques used for analysis, research, and other types of evaluation.

Each technique requires a special set of tools, such as recording templates, scripts, surveys, questionnaires, and so forth. If proactive planning extends into the *develop* phase of the ADDIE instructional design process, the practitioner selects or develops necessary confirmative evaluation tools for each technique before the training program is implemented. More often, however, the selection or development of data-collection tools begins early in the data-collection phase of the confirmative evaluation process.

Sometimes the practitioner may find generic rating forms, questionnaires, or other tools that are valid and reliable, that focus on the intended evaluation outcomes, and that fall within the budget parameters of the evaluation. At other times, the practitioner may be able to customize an existing internal or external tool to measure specific outcomes. The Toolbox at the end of this chapter lists some sources for generic or customizable evaluation instruments.

When tools are not available internally or in the marketplace, the practitioner must develop and validate guides and instruments for collecting, recording, and storing both quantitative and qualitative data. The Toolbox at the end of this chapter also lists some practitioner books that contain helpful information on how to develop surveys and questionnaires and prepare data-collection materials for group activities, interviews, and observations.

The goodness of an evaluation technique or tool is directly related to its usefulness and effectiveness from the perspective of the data collector, data source, or data analyst:

- *Data collectors* need tools such as scripts, guided interview forms, surveys, and questionnaires that help them collect complete and accurate data and make it easy to record and store quantitative and qualitative data.

- *Data sources* need structured tools such as surveys, questionnaires, or rating forms that contain clear directions and make it easy to interpret and respond to items.

- *Data analysts* need tools that collect, record, and store the data in the format that best supports the preselected evaluation design; for example, all items and ratings on a questionnaire should be coded with numbers or letters to facilitate statistical analysis.

Extant Data Analysis Techniques and Tools

Extant data analysis is the technique of identifying and reviewing existing printed or electronic documents to retrieve information that is required for assessing one or more of the intended evaluation outcomes. The practitioner, or other data collector, identifies, retrieves, and stores the required documents; documents the process; and archives or files both the original documents and the specific data retrieved from the documents for future analysis. For example, if the intended evaluation outcome is to measure the effectiveness of the training program, the data collector may collect and store performance measures (strategy documents, scorecards, business result spreadsheets, process control charts, and team or individual performance appraisal criteria or forms, to name just a few).

Extant data analysis may take place before, concurrent with, or after other data-collection efforts. The data may establish the foundation for assessing an intended evaluation outcome or be used to validate other data. For example, the data collector may review formative and summative evaluation data from a training program prior to or during the official confirmative evaluation process.

During extant data analysis, the data collector plays the role of researcher or detective, locating and retrieving data that were listed in the confirmative evaluation plan or discovering new document sources. The data collector must stay focused on the evaluation outcome(s) and have experience in locating and retrieving both print and electronic documents. He or she must also be aware of the political and even ethical realities of retrieving performance appraisals, financial reports, quality data, and other potentially sensitive documents.

Spreadsheets or other record-keeping formats help the data collector document the source of the data and record or attach the data. Sometimes entire documents may be copied and stored in a file for future use by the analyst. Electronic retrieval and storage capability makes this scenario particularly effective. At other times, the data collector may need to summarize the relevant content of the document and make available electronic or other location information so the analyst can access the document as needed. PST 5.2 is a basic form for (1) summarizing information from a document that is retrieved during extant data analysis and (2) recording the type of document, location, ownership, and the like so that the analyst may retrieve and review the complete document at a later date.

PST 5.2. Form for Recording Information During Extant Data Analysis.

Purpose: To provide sufficient information so that the data analyst can review the usefulness of the contents and retrieve the document as needed.

Directions: Complete one form for each document that is located, retrieved, or stored.

Training program:

Related evaluation outcome(s):

Related evaluation question(s):

Data collector:

Date (document retrieved and reviewed):

Title of document:

Type of document (meeting minutes, sales report, participant reaction survey, etc.):

Owner (developer, person responsible for maintaining the document, etc.):

Date of document:

Location (where the analyst can retrieve the document—for example, attached to this form or at a specific online address):

Summary of contents:

Comments:

Other:

Group Techniques and Tools

Group techniques for collecting analysis or evaluation data include brainstorming, focus groups, nominal group technique, critical incident, case studies, scenarios, and storytelling. An organization may also use quality improvement techniques that are specific to the organization's quality improvement initiative. The practitioner or a trained data collector may conduct virtual group activities or take advantage of the electronic capabilities of the organization (video conferencing, teleconferencing, Internet or Intranet e-mail, chat room, bulletin board technology, electronic whiteboard technology).

These are the basic tools required for any activity that seeks to gather information from individuals and groups:

- Guidelines to help the data collector focus and facilitate the group activity

- Forms for recording the inputs, process, outputs, and outcomes of the activity

- Directions and response forms for the participants

The tools may be in print or electronic depending on the particular group activity and the technical capability of the organization.

Interview Techniques and Tools

Interviews are traditionally considered as a one-on-one activity; however, Hale (2002a) refers to group activities, even surveys, as *interviews* and suggests: "There are four commonly used interview techniques: (1) open or unstructured; (2) structured; (3) critical-incident; and (4) surveys. What distinguishes them is (1) the amount of control each places on the interviewer and on the person being interviewed, and (2) what they measure" (p. 176). All interview techniques may be conducted in person, by telephone, or using technology such as online chat rooms, videoconferencing, and satellite broadcasts. Many organizations also have some type of groupware or meeting protocol software within their information system that is useful for conducting internal and even external (customer or supplier) interviews.

One benefit of interviews is that the interviewer can ask for clarification or probe more deeply into the interviewee's responses. A challenge is that the success of an interview is highly dependent on the people involved; the most successful interviews take place between an experienced interviewer and an interviewee who is both willing and able to share the required information.

Interviews may be structured, unstructured, or blended, depending on the type of information required. These questions illustrate the difference between structured and unstructured interviews:

- How would you rate the usefulness of the handouts provided by the trainer?

    Not sure

    Not at all useful

    Somewhat useful

    Very useful

- Do you think the handouts were useful? Why or why not?

The first question requires a specific, quantitative response and is best asked during a structured interview. The second question seeks general, qualitative feedback and is the type of question asked during an unstructured interview. If both types of questions are part of the interview protocol, it becomes a blended interview.

Hale (2002a) suggests another approach to a structured interview. Instead of providing a scale of responses for each question, the interviewer may prepare a list of anticipated answers. The interviewer then asks the question, the interviewee responds, and the interviewer classifies the response. It is important to note that this approach to a structured interview is less objective, because the *interviewer* makes assumptions about which answers to anticipate and which classification best suits a response.

A good interview requires careful thought and preparation up front. Structured interviews are fully scripted, and the interviewer follows the script during each interview to ensure the validity and reliability of multiple interviews. The script should:

- Set the interviewee at ease

- Introduce the interviewer

- Clarify the purpose and process for the interview

- List all the questions

- Provide space for the interviewer to record responses or comments (a rating scale matrix, a checklist of potential responses, a space for unanticipated or additional responses)

- Leave space for the interviewer to record personal comments

Unstructured or open interviews do not force the respondent to answer in a particular way, but the interviewer should still prepare a script that lists the questions in sequence and includes space for recording responses and comments.

Tape recorders or video set-ups are helpful during an interview; however, the interviewee must approve the use of a recording device and the interviewer should still record basic responses as a backup in case there are technical difficulties. It is also helpful if the interviewer has access to a transcription service or is experienced in transcribing audio input.

Survey Techniques and Tools

Surveys or questionnaires are especially useful for gathering qualitative data—attitudes, ideas, opinions, suggestions, and so forth. The survey items (statements) or questionnaire items (questions) are either open-ended or close-ended. Open-ended items allow the respondents to input whatever answer they feel is appropriate; close-ended items such as multiple choice or rating scales force the respondents to select a specific response. In general, the evaluation, training, or HPT practitioner should select or design closed-ended questions to collect quantitative data and open-ended items to collect qualitative data.

The main tool is the survey or questionnaire itself. Sometimes generic surveys or questionnaires are available on attitude, professional competence, and so forth. The Toolbox at the end of this chapter includes some publishers who produce generic or customized surveys or questionnaires. Still, the practitioner frequently develops the items for the confirmative evaluation because the responses sought are specific to the training program.

Wholey, Hatry, and Newcomer (1994) give a warning: "Resist the temptation to hit the ground running by rushing to write questions or to hire some consultant to draft a questionnaire. Hitting the ground is simple. It's running that requires the warm up" (p. 272). Hopefully the planners asked many or all of the questions given here during the plan phase, and the answers are recorded in the confirmative evaluation plan:

- What is the purpose of the survey?

- Who are the respondents?

- What resources are available for preparing and conducting the survey?

- What are the cultural, political, or ethical parameters?

- Will the survey collect quantitative or qualitative data, or both?

- What question type(s) should the survey contain: open, closed, or both?

- Is a pilot planned to test the survey?

An effective survey or questionnaire includes a cover letter or e-mail, which establishes rapport with the potential respondent, states the purpose for the survey or questionnaire, and motivates the respondent to complete and return the survey or questionnaire. The survey or questionnaire form itself should contain clear and unambiguous directions and a set of carefully constructed statements or questions that are logically sequenced, concise, clear, and unambiguous. The format should not be crowded, and the type size should be user-friendly.

The major responsibility for a successful survey or questionnaire lies with the practitioner, who selects or develops the instrument. PST 5.3 presents guidelines for evaluating whether a survey or questionnaire is effective for collecting the intended confirmative evaluation data.

PST 5.3. Checklist for Evaluating the Effectiveness of a Survey or Questionnaire.

Purpose: To evaluate whether a survey or questionnaire is effective for collecting intended confirmative evaluation data.

Directions: If the criteria statement in the first column is true, mark a ✓ in the box next to the statement. If a statement is not true, use the second column to write the number of the specific item(s) not meeting the criteria, or indicate what needs revision. If a criterion is not appropriate for the specific survey or questionnaire, use the second column to indicate why.

Example

Do directions meet this criteria?	If not, then revise this:
☑ Appropriately worded for target audience (age, gender, ethnic background, etc.)	
☐ Clear	#5, #6

Checklist

Does cover letter or e-mail meet these criteria?	If not, then revise this:
☐ States purpose for survey/questionnaire	
☐ Contains complete instructions for returning survey/questionnaire (date, address, etc.)	
☐ States who was selected to respond (and why)	
☐ Motivates potential respondent to complete and return the survey/questionnaire	
☐ Says "thank you" for responding	
☐ Other:	

Do directions meet these criteria?	If not, then revise this:
☐ Brief	
☐ Complete	
☐ Appropriately worded for target audience (age, gender, ethnic background, etc.)	
☐ Clear	
☐ Accurate	
☐ Unambiguous (mean what they say and say what they mean)	
☐ Provide examples (if appropriate)	
☐ Other:	

PST 5.3. Checklist for Evaluating the Effectiveness of a Survey or Questionnaire, *Continued*.

Do items (statements or questions) meet these criteria?	If not, then revise this:
☐ All items are numbered/coded for easy analysis	
☐ Items are grouped by topic if applicable	
☐ Items related to the same topic move from general to specific	
☐ Items do not suggest that one response is more appropriate than another	
☐ Items are clearly stated	
☐ Items are unambiguous (mean what they say and say what they mean)	
☐ Other:	

Do responses meet these criteria?	If not, then revise this:
☐ All responses are coded for easy analysis	
☐ Wording of scaled response is appropriate for the item	
☐ Sufficient space is available to record open-ended responses	
☐ There is a comment section (if appropriate)	
☐ Method of response is easy and appropriate for target audience	
☐ Time required to respond is appropriate for target audience	
☐ Other:	

Does format meet these criteria?	If not, then revise this:
☐ Includes as much white space as possible	
☐ Type size is appropriate for target audience	
☐ Print is dark enough for target audience	
☐ Pages are numbered "p __ of __ pages" (if appropriate)	
☐ Other:	

Observation Techniques and Tools

There is more to observing than meets the eye: "Thinking, planning, imagining, and estimating are abstract work behaviors and, one would think, unaccountable. People express the results of their work performances through observable actions, however, and the qualities of their actions can be observed. When practiced systematically, observing people at work will yield a great deal of qualitative and quantitative information about the work, the worker, and the work environment" (Swanson, 1994, p. 85).

Observation is especially appropriate for collecting confirmative evaluation data on the effectiveness, efficiency, impact, and value of visible, observable performance before and after training. Observation sounds simple, but there are many options available and it takes a trained observer to collect valid, usable data. The observer may look at the efficiency and effectiveness of a specific performance, the speed and accuracy with which a task is completed, the use of safety equipment and guidelines, the approach to troubleshooting, or the quality of the output or outcome. The challenge of using observation techniques is to "keep data collection unobtrusive [and] do everything you ethically can to obtain unsullied, representative slices of real-life behavior . . ." (Zemke and Kramlinger, 1987, p. 82).

The data collector may also combine observation with individual or group interviews (focus groups, critical incident, process mapping, storytelling, and so forth) to collect data on both physical and mental performance related to lessons learned during the training program. In addition, the observer can study the "artifacts" that are associated with a performance: a tool, product, visible stimulus such as a warning light or indicator, tracking device, work record, and so forth (Zemke and Kramlinger, 1987). The result of combining observation with other analysis techniques is what Swanson calls "a tier of information" (1994, p. 88) that is complete, accurate, and most of all useful.

The major tool for the observer is the observation guide. The most common guide is a matrix, which may include a list of activities and tasks linked to columns that allow the observer to record frequency, criticality, trigger event or stimulus, adherence to standards, accuracy, approaches to decision making or troubleshooting, and so forth. The observer may also record the performance with a video camera.

Train the Data Collectors

Effective data collection requires *experience* and *special skills.* Evaluators or training practitioners doubling as data collectors may have the necessary knowledge and skills as part of their professional repertoire. However, in a larger organization, or one where it is politically important to use local personnel as data collectors, the evaluation, training, or HPT practitioner has the added responsibility for training data collectors to ensure the validity and reliability of the data.

The Toolbox at the end of the chapter includes resources to help novice data collectors expand their knowledge and skills. The practitioner may also offer workshops, coaching or mentoring opportunities, and print or electronic PSTs. Mastering interview and group activity techniques is more time-consuming than learning how to distribute and retrieve surveys or collect documentation because interviewing and facilitating require practice. Whenever possible, select interviewers and group facilitators according to their knowledge, skill, and experience. Time and money are the major challenges to training novice data collectors.

Store the Data

How to store the data collected during the *do* phase of confirmative evaluation depends on whether the confirmative evaluation plan calls for quantitative or qualitative analysis.

In *quantitative analysis,* data collected from existing documents, surveys, observation, or interviews must be stored as frequency counts, ranks, or other quantitative measures to facilitate statistical analysis. Comments from the respondents, interviewer, facilitator, and data collector are usually stored verbatim.

In *qualitative analysis,* responses to open-ended survey items or interview questions are stored verbatim, along with any comments from the respondents or data collector. If the data collector is experienced, or the analyst collects the data, the responses may be stored within classifications or groups.

The challenge is to select, customize, or design tools for each data-collection technique that enable the data collector to record and store the responses or observations in a format that is compatible with the preselected data analysis technique.

Manage the Data-Collection Process

The confirmative evaluation plan should include a section on how to administer or manage the *do* phase of confirmative evaluation. The practitioner or the assigned project manager is responsible for:

- Allocating and tracking time, money, and personnel to monitor budgetary and other issues and priorities

- Monitoring all data-collection activities

- Preparing and distributing status reports

- Communicating with stakeholders as needed to maintain support for the confirmative evaluation

- Setting up yellow warning flags when a change could potentially delay the timely and effective completion of the *do* phase

SUMMARY: LESSONS LEARNED IN CHAPTER FIVE

1. The start-up strategy depends on whether the confirmative evaluation plan is proactive (up-front) or reactive (just-in-time).

2. The confirmative evaluation plan constitutes a blueprint for data collection.

3. There are a variety of techniques and tools to use for data collection. The key is to select the right tool and learn how to use it effectively.

4. One crucial responsibility of the data collector is to make certain that the data-collection techniques and tools are targeted on, and everyone involved in the data-collection process stays focused on, the intended evaluation outcomes and evaluation questions.

5. The major challenges faced by the data collector in my organization are:

   _____

   _____

6. Data collectors need to identify and follow professional quality standards for program evaluation.

7. Personal lessons learned:

   _____

   _____

   _____

NEXT STEPS

The next step is to analyze and interpret the data and to report the results of the confirmative evaluation. The authors have separated the *do* and *analyze* phases of confirmative evaluation to emphasize the importance of both activities, as well as how the goodness of data collection affects the goodness of the analysis, interpretation, and reporting activities. However, if the same person serves as both data collector and analyst, then the activities discussed in this and the following chapter may occur concurrently.

TOOLBOX FOR DATA COLLECTION

These professional books and publishers offer resources for selecting, customizing, developing, and using data-collection techniques and tools.

Professional Books

Combs, W. L., and Falletta, S. V. *The Targeted Evaluation Process: A Consultant's Guide to Asking the Right Questions and Getting the Results You Trust.* Alexandria, Va.: American Society for Training and Development, 2000. (See Chapter Nine of that book, on designing the tools, technology, and techniques, for a practical discussion of how to select, design, or customize tools; use technology; and achieve reliability and validity.)

Dixon, N. M. *Evaluation: A Tool for Improving HRD Quality.* San Francisco: Pfeiffer; Alexandria, Va.: American Society for Training and Development, 1990. (Part Five of that book contains chapters on collecting and analyzing data from interviews and surveys, including a chapter on validity.)

Fuller, J. *Managing Performance Improvement Projects.* San Francisco: Jossey-Bass/Pfeiffer and International Society for Performance Improvement (ISPI), 1997. (Features steps and suggestions for managing a successful performance improvement project.)

Hale, J. *Performance-Based Evaluation: Tools and Techniques to Measure the Impact of Training.* San Francisco: Jossey-Bass/Pfeiffer, 2002. (Chapter Ten of that book contains practical information on how to collect data using observation; document searches; and individual or group processes such as critical incident analysis, focus groups, nominal group technique, process mapping, and surveys.)

Rossett, A. *Training Needs Assessment.* Englewood Cliffs, N.J.: Educational Technology Publications, 1987. (Includes chapters on extant data analysis, interviewing, observing, working with groups, and writing questionnaires and surveys.)

Rossett, A. *First Things Fast.* San Francisco: Jossey-Bass/Pfeiffer, 1999. (Contains chapters on interviews, focus groups, observations, surveys, and using technology to collect data.)

Swanson, R. A. *Analysis for Improving Performance.* San Francisco: Berrett-Koehler, 1994. (Chapter Seven of that book is an overview of a number of techniques: interviews, questionnaires, observations, and reviewing organizational records.)

TOOLBOX FOR DATA COLLECTION, *Continued*

Wholey, J. S., Hatry, H. P., and Newcomer, K. E. (eds.). *Handbook of Practical Program Evaluation*. San Francisco: Jossey-Bass, 1994. (Part Two of that book includes chapters on collecting data from observation, surveys, role plays, focus groups, existing records, and field experiments.)

Zemke, R., and Kramlinger, T. *Figuring Things Out: A Trainer's Guide to Needs and Task Analysis*. Reading, Mass.: Addison-Wesley, 1987. (Contains chapters on observation, focus groups, telephone and face-to-face interviews, critical incident, consensus groups, and surveys and questionnaires.)

Publishers

Goal/QPC: *Memory Jogger Pocket Guides* and other quality-based tools and techniques; (800) 643-4316 or www.goalqpc.com

HRD Press: generic assessment instruments; (800) 822-2801 or www.hrdpress.com

HRDQ: generic assessment instruments; (800) 633-4533 or www.hrdq.com

Human Synergistics: generic assessment instruments; (800) 622-7584 or www.humansyn.com

Pfeiffer *Annuals*: Elaine Biech edits a yearly compendium that contains sample inventories and surveys; (800) 274-4434 or www.Pfeiffer.com

Psychological Corporation: generic assessment instruments; (800) 872-1726 or www.PsychCorp.com

QuestionMark: software for writing, administering, and reporting on assessments, tests, surveys; (800) 863-3950 or www.questionmark.com

Sage Publications: professional books on evaluation and research; (805) 499-0721 or www.sagepub.com

Teleometrics: generic assessment instruments; (800) 527-0406 or www.teleometrics.com

Training Technologies: electronic survey tracker; (513) 754-1212, www.traintech.com, or www.surveytracker.com

Web-Based Resource

Refereed checklists and other resources for collecting evaluation data are available at www.wmich.edu/evalctr/checklists

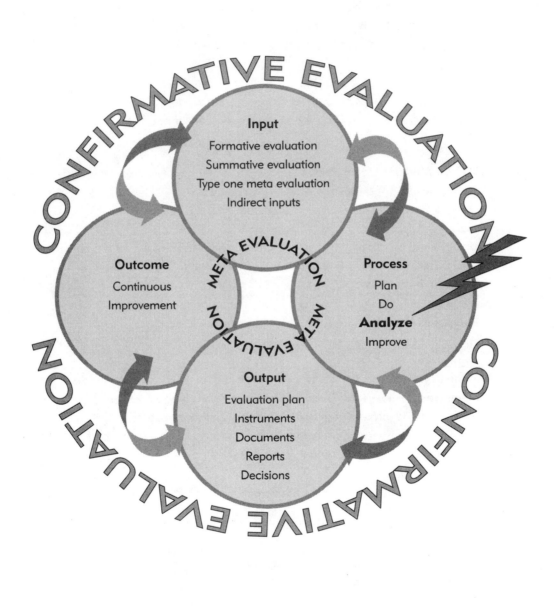

CONFIRMATIVE EVALUATION

CONFIRMATIVE EVALUATION

Input
Formative evaluation
Summative evaluation
Type one meta evaluation
Indirect inputs

Process
Plan
Do
Analyze
Improve

Outcome
Continuous
Improvement

Output
Evaluation plan
Instruments
Documents
Reports
Decisions

META EVALUATION

META EVALUATION

6

Analyze: Everything Old Is New Again

ONCE CONFIRMATIVE EVALUATION DATA are collected by surveys, questionnaires, interviews, observations, or group activities, they need to be analyzed, interpreted, and communicated. During the *analysis* phase, the evaluation, training, or HPT practitioner takes on the role of analyst, stays focused on the confirmative evaluation outcomes and evaluation questions, and strives to:

- Analyze: organize the data and discover what they mean

- Interpret: find out which results are significant, why they are significant, and what implications the significance has for the next phase of the confirmative evaluation process (*improve*)

- Communicate: share the findings plus the analysis and interpretation results with the stakeholders who need the information to improve performance

The goodness of analysis and interpretation depends on the goodness of the data and the knowledge and skills of the analyst.

This chapter contains practical suggestions and guidelines on how to analyze and interpret data and communicate the confirmative evaluation results. We differentiate between quantitative and qualitative data analysis, focus on analyzing and interpreting the confirmative evaluation results, spend some time outlining what constitutes an effective confirmative evaluation report, and present a Toolbox of professional books and software packages to jumpstart the analysis and communication process.

After reading this chapter, you will be able to:

1. Identify generic methods for analyzing quantitative and qualitative confirmative evaluation data

2. Identify generic software packages for analyzing quantitative and qualitative confirmative evaluation data

3. Discuss what is involved in interpreting confirmative evaluation data

4. Identify generic methods useful for interpreting confirmative evaluation data

5. Describe how to communicate confirmative evaluation results and recommendations

6. Suggest an appropriate outline, style, and structure for a confirmative evaluation report

Get Ready, Get Set

During the analysis process, the practitioner works with whatever data were collected during the *do* phase of confirmative evaluation, to determine which intended evaluation outcomes the data support and whether these data are solid enough to support drawing conclusions and making decisions. At times, the analyst may need to review and even revise the confirmative evaluation plan (type of data, analysis strategy, communication plan, and so forth) to ensure that the intended outcomes of the confirmative evaluation can be achieved. For the time being, however, let the analysis begin.

Sources from the literature on program evaluation (such as Brinkerhoff, Brethower, Hluchyj, and Nowakowski, 1983; Phillips, 1997b; Russ-Eft and

Preskill, 2001; Windsor, Baranowski, Clark, and Cutter, 1994; and many others) offer basic guidelines for analyzing evaluation data. Here are some general heuristics or rules of thumb that are particularly important when analyzing confirmative evaluation data:

- Stay focused on the intended confirmative evaluation outcomes and evaluation questions.

- Track variables carefully, and be alert for unanticipated results.

- Make sure you can support all your conclusions and recommendations with relevant, accurate, and consistent data.

- Keep analysis as simple, practical, and economical as possible, while making sure it is sufficient to achieve the intended evaluation outcomes.

- Never assume stakeholders understand what you do during the analysis phase.

- Follow ethical standards related to analysis, including standards related to confidentiality, use of human subjects, statistical processing of data, and so forth.

Prepare the Confirmative Evaluation Data

There are three steps the analyst should perform prior to beginning the actual analysis:

1. Retrieve the data that were collected and stored during the *do* phase of confirmative evaluation.

2. Organize the data to meet the requirements of the preselected analysis method.

3. Inspect the data to determine goodness.

Retrieve the Data

Sometimes the analyst is also the data collector; sometimes the analyst comes on the scene after data collectors have collected and stored the data in print or electronic form. In the second scenario, the analyst must retrieve the data and begin to organize them into a useful format. In either case, it is vital that all the data be properly stored, storage locations be well documented, and the analyst have easy access to the data. In short, the data should be organized to be logical, safe, and easy to retrieve.

Organize the Data

If the data are not analysis-ready, the analyst must organize the data to meet the requirements of the selected analysis method. This may entail aggregating, grouping, or coding the data:

• *Aggregate.* Sometimes data related to the same outcome or confirmative evaluation question are collected from a number of sources and stored in different locations. The analyst must identify and retrieve the data from the various stored sources and put the data together in a usable format for analysis.

• *Group.* Sometimes the analyst needs to collapse the data and look at intervals or classes. This means the analyst must identify and retrieve all the data that belong within each interval or class and put the data together in a usable format for analysis. If the data-collection tools were properly designed, similar items are already grouped together. (See Chapter Five for a discussion of data-collection tools.)

• *Code.* Coding is essential when the confirmative evaluation plan calls for quantitative analysis methods. In the best-case scenario, each item, rank, or response on the surveys, questionnaires, rating forms, and other data-collection tools is identified with a number or letter (code). If items are not coded, the analyst must develop and apply a code prior to analysis, which is not as accurate or easy to work with as a preset code. The goal is a simple but complete coding system that makes data analysis easier and more accurate; all data from surveys and other instruments are recorded in one computerized record, making the data easy to record, tabulate, scan, store, and retrieve.

Inspect the Data

While or after the data are organized, the analyst should consider whether the data that have been collected are worth analyzing. The analyst has several options—eyeball methods, spot checks, audits, group meetings of analyzers, or accuracy ratings—to help guarantee that the data are robust and sensitive to the needs of the organization and the stakeholders. For example, did any of these conditions result in invalid or otherwise useless data?

- Partially completed instruments
- Multiple coding errors
- Respondents not representative of the population
- Respondents not randomized
- Monitoring and administration procedures inconsistent with implementation guidelines

Now Analyze

Once the data are organized, the analyst may begin to analyze them according to the procedures established in the confirmative evaluation plan. The analyst needs to remain focused on the purpose of conducting the specific analysis. This means refocusing on the specific confirmative evaluation outcome or confirmative evaluation question that is being analyzed at the time.

It is important and politically astute to involve the stakeholders in the data analysis process. The analyst gains insight into the questions raised, is sensitized to the trigger points of the stakeholders, and becomes aware of opportunities for exploring new issues. The stakeholders, on the other hand, realize that statistics can be friendly, that statistics reduce data to a briefer form, and that their involvement is necessary and appreciated (Patton, 1987). One way to involve stakeholders in the analysis phase of confirmative evaluation is to establish a blue-ribbon committee of stakeholders for reviewing data analysis procedures, methodologies, and practices. Whatever involvement strategy the analyst selects, including stakeholders in the analysis process goes a long way toward establishing buy-in and educating the stakeholders about the analysis process itself.

Quantitative Data Analysis

Quantitative data include weights or rankings, frequency counts, scores, and so forth, "expressed in whole numbers, fractions, decimals, or percentages" (Hale, 2002a, p. 227). The purpose of quantitative data analysis is to describe data in terms of central tendency or dispersion, search for or predict relationships among variables, and test for significant differences among variables.

The analyst does not have to be an expert in statistics to perform quantitative analysis. However, the analyst does need to have a basic understanding of statistical theory and procedures and be familiar with the selected statistical methods in order to conduct the analysis; explain the inputs, process, outputs, and outcomes to the stakeholders; and help the stakeholders interpret the analysis results.

Table 6.1 gives an overview of some of the major statistical analysis methods you can use if you must describe confirmative evaluation data, search for or predict relationships, or test for significance. Hopefully, the statistical method was selected in the *plan* phase and the selection was soundly based on what you need to find out to achieve the intended evaluation outcomes and answer the targeted evaluation questions. Now all you have to do is analyze the data!

The Toolbox at the end of this chapter refers you to more in-depth and user-friendly information on quantitative analysis methodology, including a

Table 6.1. Options for Analyzing Quantitative Data.

Purpose	Statistical Analysis Options
Describe the data	• Mean, median, or mode (measures of central tendency) • Range or standard deviation (measures of dispersion)
Search for relationships	• Correlation analysis (two variables) • Factor or cluster analysis (three or more variables)
Predict relationships	• Regression or discriminant analysis (two variables) • Multiple regression or discriminant analysis (three or more variables)
Test significance	• Chi square • ANOVA (analysis of variance) • ANCOVA (analysis of covariance) • t-test

list of statistical software packages that are designed to store, categorize, code, sort, and analyze data. A simple word-processing program is sufficient for small confirmative evaluation projects; a software suite that includes word-processing, database, and spreadsheet programs is preferable for large projects.

Qualitative Data Analysis

Qualitative data analysis is becoming an accepted component of evaluation and research. Qualitative data add distinct elements of richness and sensitivity to the results of data analysis. On the process side of analysis, "because they are 'personalized,' qualitative methods [surveys, interviews, focus groups, and so forth] may add emotion and tone to purely statistical findings . . ." (Fink, 1993, p. 11).

Qualitative data are "concepts, ideas, opinions, conclusions, preferences, and so on that are expressed orally or in writing through words, phrases, stories, or narrative passages" (Hale, 2002a, p. 228). The purpose of qualitative data analysis is to identify "themes and patterns in the data and then code and categorize these themes in an effort to understand and explain the phenomenon being evaluated" (Russ-Eft and Preskill, 2001, p. 319). Within the framework of confirmative evaluation, the practitioner derives categories from stakeholder information needs as they are ultimately expressed in the intended evaluation outcomes and the targeted evaluation questions.

The Toolbox at the end of this chapter includes user-friendly professional books that present more in-depth information on when, why, and how to analyze qualitative data. There is also a list of qualitative analysis software that serves as "an electronic facilitator of text-based analysis, helping the researcher to parse [break down] the data and explore relationships between responses" (Rossett, 1999, p. 131).

Cost Analysis

Cost analysis is an umbrella term for a set of analysis techniques that compare program costs with program benefits, effectiveness, utility, or feasibility. Cost analysis is difficult and time-consuming. However, it is crucial for decision making in today's cost-conscious and bottom-line-oriented business world, where it is becoming increasingly important to base decisions related to training and other performance improvement interventions on the business value of the intervention. When we say *business value* we are referring to "the continuing competence of the performers who participate in the interventions and the continuing effectiveness of the entire performance improvement package including products and processes" (Van Tiem, Moseley, and Dessinger, 2000, pp. 176–177) as well as the cost associated with implementing or not implementing the intervention.

Traditionally, cost-benefit and cost-effectiveness analyses are conducted after a program is implemented and relate directly to confirmative evaluation; cost-feasibility and cost-utility analyses are most often used prior to program implementation, but the confirmative evaluation plan may include activities for validating the results of an up-front cost-utility or cost-feasibility analysis.

Cost-Benefit Analysis. Cost-benefit analysis (CBA), sometimes known as benefit-cost analysis, is a practical quantitative procedure that the confirmative evaluation analyst can use to compare the cost of the training program with the benefits resulting from the program: "A program may have been instituted for a complex set of political and other external reasons and it becomes important to have hard data on its impact and the ratio of benefits to costs . . ." (Rossi and Freeman, 1993, p. 45).

During cost-benefit analysis, the practitioner identifies all the obvious and hidden costs of planning, designing, implementing, and evaluating the training program and all the individual, group, business, or organizational benefits that resulted from the training program; he or she then assigns a dollar value to each cost *and* benefit. "The evaluator can then calculate the net benefits (or costs) of the program; examine the ratio of benefits to costs; determine the rate of return on the original investment; and compare the program's benefits and costs with those of other programs or proposed alternatives"(Kee, 1994, p. 456).

It is often difficult and challenging to identify the unit of analysis for both costs and benefits, assign the appropriate monetary value for benefits, and discover hidden costs. For example, a hidden cost might be a decrease in productivity when a work group member is attending the training program; the benefit might be increased productivity directly related to the training program outcomes. The Toolbox at the end of this chapter suggests some professional books on how to conduct cost-benefit analysis of programs, including training programs.

Cost-Effectiveness Analysis. According to Kee (1994), cost-effectiveness analysis is "the major costing alternative to benefit-cost analysis"; the output is a ratio that "relates the cost of a given alternative to specific measures of program objectives . . . for example, dollars per life saved" (p. 457). Cost-effectiveness analysis can help stakeholders compare training programs and delivery systems (classroom versus self-study, satellite broadcast versus computer-based training, and so forth). Cost-effectiveness analysis also reduces the difficulty of trying to place a monetary value on training benefits. This is particularly important when a training program is long-term and there are volumes of data to collect and convert.

Cost-Utility Analysis. Cost-utility analysis is another method for analyzing alternative training programs. Cost-utility analysis is a subjective analysis of the cost and estimated utility or usefulness of the outcomes of a program. This makes it difficult to establish the basis for analysis and even more difficult to defend the results (Worthen, Sanders, and Fitzpatrick, 1997).

Here is an example: an analyst calculates the costs of each of three training programs on cold calling presented by three vendors. Then the analyst estimates that salespeople who complete any of the programs will increase their monthly sales by X percent. The analyst also estimates that the increase in sales will have a scaled value of 4 (on a scale of 5 = very high to 1 = very low) for the sales departments involved. The analyst then multiplies the probability of achieving the increase in sales by the estimated value of the increase. Now the analyst has two points of comparison: cost and estimated utility. The analyst can also apply cost-utility analysis to a single training program that is offered at multiple locations over months or years, or to analyze the cost utility of a training program with multiple outcomes.

Cost-Feasibility Analysis. Cost-feasibility analysis is usually conducted up front to determine whether to implement a program; however, sometimes decision makers are faced with shrinking budgets and need to know whether it is still expedient, or even possible financially, to continue a training program. Cost-feasibility analysis is strictly a matter of calculating and comparing the costs of the program with the department or division budget. Conducting a feasibility analysis during confirmative evaluation can help decision makers determine whether the original feasibility study was accurate or whether they can continue to maintain the program.

Return on Investment (ROI) Analysis

Since 1959, organizations have been using Kirkpatrick's four levels of evaluation: immediate reaction, immediate learning, on-the-job behavior, and results. Almost forty years later, Phillips, Pulliam, and Wurtz (1998), noting the increased impact of the bottom line on healthy organizations, added a fifth level: return on investment (ROI).

ROI is the cost-analysis technique most closely related to confirmative evaluation. However, there is a danger of equating ROI with confirmative evaluation and thus missing out on the broad inputs and purposes of full-scope evaluation. ROI is *not* the same as confirmative evaluation; it is an additional measurement of success, and a crucial one for evaluating long-term training programs.

ROI ≠ Confirmative Evaluation

Basic ROI analysis is similar to CBA. Both techniques place a monetary value on the costs and benefits of a training program and come up with a cost-to-benefit ratio. However, ROI goes a step further by subtracting program costs from program benefits to calculate the net benefits, dividing the net benefits by the program costs, and multiplying by 100. The result is an ROI percentage that may be low for hard skills or technical training but go beyond 100 percent for soft skills training such as sales (Phillips, 1997b).

During confirmative evaluation, the ROI analysis must include all the design, development, implementation, and evaluation costs of the program, from design through implementation and maintenance, as well as the long-term hidden costs (such as expenses) that occur each time participants leave work and attend the training. The ROI analysis must also focus on the intended outcomes of the training program—effectiveness, efficiency, impact, and value—to determine the benefits.

Phillips, Pulliam, and Wurtz (1998) and others report that business buzz-words such as "accountability," "alignment," "three Rs" (restructure, reengineer, rightsizing), and "quality" imply an increasing interest in and need for ROI analysis. Organizations call out for evaluation, training, and HPT practitioners to show where the money goes; prove there's a link between business and performance needs; or measure continuous quality improvement. For specific information on how to analyze ROI in your organization, refer to the resources in the Toolbox at the end of the chapter.

Add Risk Analysis to the Mix

Jackson (1989) suggests that the most effective way to predict or confirm the benefits or success of a training program, or compare alternative programs, is to *combine* risk analysis with CBA or ROI analysis. Risk analysis establishes the expected value of a training program and the probability of success and then makes it possible to analyze whether the actual value is equal to the expected value. The stage is set for risk analysis during proactive confirmative evaluation planning, because the success of the risk analysis results depends on up-front activities such as cost-feasibility analysis, clear definition of program objectives, and alignment of program objectives with performance criteria.

For further discussion of alignment, see Chapter Seven. For generic information on using risk analysis, see the Toolbox at the end of this chapter.

Interpret Confirmative Evaluation Results

Only a few authors (for example, Worthen, Sanders, and Fitzpatrick, 1997) treat interpretation as a separate activity with a distinct methodology. In this book, we consider interpretation as part of the *analyze* phase, yet distinct enough to be discussed separately.

During data analysis, the role of the analyst is to use ". . . a set of statistical [and other] tools that reduce the amount of detail in the data, summarizing it and making the most important facts and relationships apparent" (Alreck and Settle, 1995, p. 267). Then it's time for interpretation. The analyst focuses on the results, discovers what the results really mean, and draws results-based conclusions that meet stakeholder information needs, support the intended evaluation outcomes, answer the targeted questions, and are useful for recommending further action.

PST 6.1 is a checklist of questions the analyst may ask during data interpretation. The Toolbox at the end of this chapter includes some professional books on data interpretation.

PST 6.1. Checklist for Interpreting Confirmative Evaluation Results.

Purpose: To help identify what analysis results really mean.

Directions: After you have completed analyzing the confirmative evaluation data, review the analysis results. Then use the items below to guide your interpretation of the results. Adapt the checklist to your specific needs: place a ✓ before any question below that you feel you need to ask during the interpretation stage, or any item that needs further verification, or just to indicate that you are satisfied with the answer to the question and are ready to move on. Add additional questions that are specific to the data you are working with.

☐ Do the results support the intended outcome(s) established in the confirmative evaluation plan?

☐ Do the results answer the targeted evaluation question(s) established in the confirmative evaluation plan?

☐ Do the results meet stakeholder needs?

☐ Do the results meet stakeholder expectations?

☐ Are there weaknesses in the analysis techniques or tools that skewed the results?

☐ Are the results valid (sound)?

☐ Are the results reliable (consistent)?

☐ Are the results useful?

☐ Are the results valuable?

☐ Are there similar results from other evaluations that I can use to verify these results?

☐ Other:

No matter how objective the interpreter tries to be, interpretation is a personal activity. The Victorian poet Alfred, Lord Tennyson, wrote: "I am a part of all that I have met." So it is with the practitioner who is responsible for interpreting data. He or she brings personal life experiences to the interpretation landscape as well as technical skills, practical savvy, and conceptual abilities, all of which cannot help but color the landscape and affect the perspective. If the analyst also involves the stakeholders in interpreting the data, the perspective becomes even broader and, although objectivity may waver, the potential for buy-in is stronger.

Make Results-Based Recommendations

Once interpretation is completed, the analyst uses the results to make solid reality-based recommendations for future action. The analyst should consider these factors when making recommendations:

- Are the recommendations aligned with the specific commitments to action that the stakeholders made during the confirmative evaluation planning sessions?

- Are the recommendations aligned with the organization's mission and values?

- Will the current or future organizational climate and culture support the recommendations?

- Are sufficient resources available to implement the recommendations (time, money, personnel, and so forth)?

- What type of change-management effort is required to implement the recommendations?

- What are the benefits, barriers, risks, and rewards for implementing the recommendations?

The Toolbox at the end of the chapter suggests books that further the discussion of what issues to take into account when making recommendations.

Report Confirmative Evaluation Results

When does the evaluator end the analysis process and decide to report the results to the stakeholders? According to Brinkerhoff, Brethower, Hluchyj, and Nowakowski: "With quantitative data, you arrive at a level of certainty you're willing to defend; with qualitative data, you encounter redundancy, or regularity. . . . You never conclude analysis. You stop doing it" (1983, p. 146). Here are some tips on what to do when you decide to stop. There are additional resources on writing evaluation reports in the Toolbox at the end of this chapter.

Communicate, Communicate, Communicate

The evaluation literature (including Russ-Eft and Preskill, 2001) stresses that reporting confirmative evaluation results is not a one-time-only function; nor is it one-way communication. Communicating with stakeholders should be a continuous, collaborative process with ongoing dialogue where stakeholders are totally involved in such decisions as the purpose, content, design, presentation, logistics, and timing of the confirmative evaluation report. However, even if the practitioner maintains active communication with stakeholders throughout the confirmative evaluation process, it is still good knowledge-management practice to produce a single, archivable final report.

Consider Style, Format, and Content

The style of the final report is on a continuum from formal to informal, depending on the organization and the audience. The format may vary, in accordance with organizational standards and resources—hard copy, electronic, or a presentation with handouts. However, the one constant is the content: a clear, concise, and focused summary of the *entire* analyze phase—who did what when, what happened, and why, with recommendations for action.

The content of the final report depends on who needs to know what and why. The confirmative evaluation plan should address answers to several questions, but since time may have elapsed between *plan* and *do* the report writer should do a current reality check:

- Who needs to know?

- What information should each person know?

- Why do they have to know (what are the intended evaluation outcomes and targeted evaluation questions)?

- What problems are likely to occur from the results of data analysis,
  the interpretation of the results, or the recommendations for action?

PST 6.2 is a general outline for a formal final report; it may be adapted to
informal reports as well. For a sample evaluation report, see the reference to
Boulmetis and Dutwin (2000) in the Toolbox at the end of this chapter.

PST 6.2. Outline for a Formal Confirmative Evaluation Final Report.

Purpose: To help identify what to include in a formal confirmative evaluation final report, and to serve as a guideline for writing the report.

Directions: Use this outline to plan a formal confirmative evaluation final report or adjust the outline if your organization requires a less formal presentation.

1. **Executive summary**

2. **Table of contents**

3. **Introduction:** purpose, intended evaluation outcome, targeted evaluation questions, audience, and scope, at a minimum

4. **Background information:** historical data, including summary of *plan* phase, challenges, limitations, special circumstances, and so forth

5. **Body of report:** summary of what happened during *do* (data collection) and *analyze* (data analysis and interpretation)—inputs, process, outputs, and outcomes

6. **Summary:** conclusions and recommendations

7. **Closing:** benefits of conducting the confirmative evaluation, limitations, special implications, lessons learned, and so on

8. **Appendices:** data-collection instruments, graphics (if not placed in the body of the report), budget, timeline, and the like

Use Communication Tools Wisely and Well

Communication tools are frequently built into analysis tools. For example, a statistical software package may analyze the data and present the results in a chart or other graphic that may be imported into a word processing program or slide presentation program. There are also a variety of word processing and graphics software packages on the market that make it relatively easy for the analyst to prepare a graphic display of data visually interpreting the results of the confirmative evaluation. The writer should be savvy about working with these tools and about using figures, graphs, charts, diagrams, tables, or other graphics to display (1) quantitative data resulting from the analysis of central tendencies, dispersion, frequency distributions, and score comparisons; and (2) qualitative data resulting from theme and pattern, content, or summary analyses. The Toolbox at the end of this chapter lists some analysis software that contains communication tools.

Inform and Inspire

At this point in the confirmative evaluation process, communication should be part information and part inspiration. The final report should contain all the information the stakeholders need to know while inspiring them to take action. Above all, whoever communicates the results of the confirmative evaluation should remember to celebrate the successes of the evaluation and suggest positive solutions for any negative outcomes. The goal is to motivate the reader to take considered action for continuous improvement supported by solid confirmative evaluation results.

SUMMARY: LESSONS LEARNED IN CHAPTER SIX

1. Analysis and interpretation are different activities. Analysis reduces information to useable formats and makes inferences; interpretation derives meaning so you can draw conclusions.

2. Analysis is a never-ending process. The analyst just knows when to stop.

3. Quantitative data should be complemented by qualitative data.

4. Quantitative and qualitative data analysis software packages help make the analysis process mystery-free and user-friendly.

5. Continuous communication with stakeholders is an important part of the confirmative evaluation process.

6. The final confirmative evaluation report summarizes inputs, processes, outputs, and outcomes for stakeholders in the style and format that best suit their needs.

7. Personal lessons learned:

_____

_____

_____

_____

_____

_____

_____

_____

NEXT STEPS

The final step in the confirmative evaluation process is *improve*. The next chapter focuses on the importance of continuous improvement and the changing and challenging roles of the evaluation, training, or HPT practitioner.

TOOLBOX FOR ANALYSIS, INTERPRETATION, AND REPORTING

Here are professional books and publishers offering resources for analyzing and interpreting data and communicating confirmative evaluation results. The resources are generic because very little is written in the literature about analyzing data specifically for confirmative evaluation purposes. The purpose may vary among the types of evaluation, but analysis techniques remain basically the same.

Professional Books

Boulmetis, J., and Dutwin, P. *The ABCs of Evaluation: Timeless Techniques for Program and Project Managers*. San Francisco: Jossey-Bass, 2000. (Chapter Seven in that book, on data analysis, and Chapter Nine, on writing the evaluation report, are particularly relevant. The book also contains a useful appendix on data analysis and a sample evaluation report.)

Brinkerhoff, R. O., Brethower, D. M., Hluchyj, T., and Nowakowski, J. R. *Program Evaluation: A Practitioner's Guide for Trainers and Educators*. Boston: Kluwer-Nijhoff, 1983. (Offers guidance on interpreting data analyses.)

Combs, W. L., and Falletta, S. V. *The Targeted Evaluation Process: A Performance Consultant's Guide to Asking the Right Questions and Getting the Results You Trust*. Alexandria, Va.: American Society for Training and Development, 2000. (Chapter Eleven in that book, "Reporting Results," discusses how to make recommendations, prepare the report, and present the report.)

Hale, J. *Performance-Based Evaluation: Tools and Techniques to Measure the Impact of Training*. San Francisco: Jossey-Bass/Pfeiffer, 2002. (Chapter Eleven in that book, on how to analyze data using descriptive statistics, and Chapter Twelve, on how to analyze data using inferential statistics, are very useful. Page 229 presents information on qualitative analysis.)

Jackson, T. *Evaluation: Relating Training to Business Performance*. San Francisco: Pfeiffer, 1989. (Chapter Five in that book, "Calculating the Benefits," explains the use of cost-benefit analysis, risk analysis, and ROI.)

The Joint Committee on Standards for Educational Evaluation. *The Program Evaluation Standards: How to Assess Evaluation of Educational Programs* (2nd ed.). Thousand Oaks, Calif.: Sage, 1994. (Practical and ethical guidance on conducting all evaluation activities.)

TOOLBOX FOR ANALYSIS, INTERPRETATION, AND REPORTING, *Continued*

Shadish, W. R., Newman, D. L., Scheirer, M. A., and Wye, C. (Eds.). *Guiding Principles for Evaluators,* New Directions for Program Evaluation, No. 66, San Francisco: Jossey-Bass, 1995. (Discusses the American Evaluation Association [AEA] *Guiding Principles for Evaluators.*)

Morris, L. L., and Fitz-Gibbon, C. T. *How to Present an Evaluation Report.* Thousand Oaks, Calif.: Sage, 1978. (The entire monograph is a practical guide on how to present an evaluation report to various stakeholders as effectively and painlessly as possible.)

Rossett, A. *First Things Fast.* San Francisco: Jossey-Bass/Pfeiffer, 1999. (Chapter Eight in that book, "Communicating Results," discusses how to communicate the results of a performance analysis and includes a sample report and presentation. Many suggestions are also applicable to communicating evaluation results. In addition, some of the statistical software packages on pages 125 and 126 offer graphic elements for import into word-processing or presentation programs.)

Russ-Eft, D., and Preskill, H. *Evaluation in Organizations: A Systematic Approach to Enhancing Learning, Performance, and Change.* Cambridge, Mass.: Perseus, 2001. (Refer to Chapter Twelve in that book, "Analyzing Evaluation Data," and Chapter Thirteen, "Communicating and Reporting Evaluation Activities and Findings." The authors also discuss qualitative analysis on pages 324 and 325 and suggest software packages for quantitative and qualitative analysis on page 341.)

Wholey, J. S. "Assessing the Feasibility and Likely Usefulness of Evaluation." In J. S. Wholey, H. P. Hatry, and K. E. Newcomer (eds.), *Handbook of Practical Program Evaluation.* San Francisco: Jossey-Bass, 1994. (Discusses why and when to include, and how to analyze, feasibility and utilization data.)

Worthen, B. R., Sanders, J. R., and Fitzpatrick, J. L. *Program Evaluation: Alternative Approaches and Practical Guidelines* (2nd ed.). White Plains, N.Y.: Longman, 1997. (Gives guidance on interpreting data analyses.)

Publisher

Sage Publications: (805) 499-0721, or www.sagepub.com; offers a range of professional books on data analysis for evaluation and research

TOOLBOX FOR ANALYSIS, INTERPRETATION, AND REPORTING, *Continued*

Quantitative Analysis Software Packages

Excel (spreadsheet package) (www.microsoft.com)
JMP (general statistical package) (www.sas.com)
MiniTab (DOS and Windows): Minitab, Inc. (www.minitab.com)
SAS/STAT (www.sas.com)
SPSS, Statistical Package for the Social Sciences (www.spss.com)
StartView: Abacus Concepts (www.abacus.com)
Winks Professional Ed (www.texasoft.com)

Qualitative Analysis Software Package (for Large Projects)

NUD*IST (Non-Numerical Unstructured Data Indexing, Searching and Theory-building; www.sagepub.com)

Presentation Software

Powerpoint (www.microsoft.com)

Web-Based Resource

Refereed checklists and other resources for analyzing and reporting evaluation information are available at www.wmich.edu/evalctr/checklists

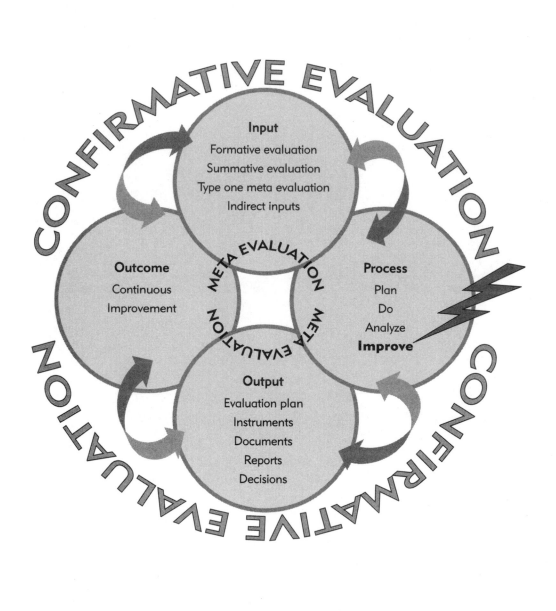

CONFIRMATIVE EVALUATION
CONFIRMATIVE EVALUATION

Input
Formative evaluation
Summative evaluation
Type one meta evaluation
Indirect inputs

META EVALUATION
META EVALUATION

Process
Plan
Do
Analyze
Improve

Outcome
Continuous
Improvement

Output
Evaluation plan
Instruments
Documents
Reports
Decisions

7

Improve: Now What?

FROM GEIS AND SMITH (1992) to Fitzpatrick, Sanders, and Worthen (2004) and beyond, the literature strongly links good evaluation to good performance improvement. When an organization plans and implements a full-scope evaluation and stakeholders commit to actions based on confirmative evaluation outcomes, the organization is saying that it cares about continuous improvement and wants to make sure continuous improvement happens. At this point, we can say that the confirmative evaluation is *utilization-focused*, which means that the evaluation planners have designed an evaluation that will generate outcomes the stakeholders may use to improve performance (Patton, 1997).

So, what happens next? Does the role of the practitioner end once the final report is communicated and approved? The internal evaluator may be constrained by organization-determined roles or else have the freedom to suggest expanding his or her role beyond traditional evaluation activities (Hodges, 2002). The role of an external evaluation, training, or HPT practitioner working in a continuous improvement initiative is also dependent on cultural, economic, political, logistical, contractual, and related issues.

This chapter emphasizes that taking action to improve performance or quality is an integral part of the confirmative evaluation process; it also emphasizes that the evaluation, training, or (especially) HPT practitioner should take an active part in the *improve* phase. Improvement efforts may focus on the training program; the individual, business, or organization; or the confirmative evaluation itself. Improvement implies change, and change implies risk taking, so the improve phase is a challenging and risky venture.

After reading this chapter, you will be able to:

1. Explain the concept of *utilization evaluation*

2. Describe the foci of the improve phase of confirmative evaluation

3. Recognize the role of meta evaluation in establishing credibility and accountability

4. Recognize the various roles and responsibilities of the practitioner during the improve phase of confirmative evaluation

5. Identify the challenges to using confirmative evaluation to improve performance and quality

Focus on Utilization

Effective confirmative evaluation is utilization-focused (Combs and Falletta, 2000; Patton, 1997; The Joint Committee on Standards for Educational Evaluation, 1994; and others). Focusing on how the stakeholders and the practitioner will use the intended outcomes during the *improve* phase should drive decisions made during the *plan, do,* and *analyze* phases. For example, the confirmative evaluation planning process flowchart in PST 3.1 (Chapter Three) illustrates that the final decision to develop a confirmative evaluation plan is dependent on whether the stakeholders will commit to take action based on the confirmative evaluation outcomes.

The need to improve drives the stakeholder information needs that drive the confirmative evaluation outcomes that drive the entire evaluation effort.

Traditionally, the *improve* phase of the confirmative evaluation model aims at improving the performance and quality of the training program. However, enlightened decision makers look beyond training and development to continuously improve the performance of the individual, group, business, or organization, and the quality of processes, products, or services. In turn, enlightened practitioners turn the spotlight inward to focus on continuous improvement of both the training program and the confirmative evaluation itself.

Improve the Training Program

Traditionally, confirmative evaluation focuses on improving the efficiency, effectiveness, impact, or value of a training program. Table 7.1 illustrates the options available to those decision makers who are responsible for determining the future of a training program according to how well it responds to stakeholder needs. The decision makers may decide to maintain the training program as is, revise it, discard it, or replace it with an existing or new program. The intended outcomes of the confirmative evaluation certainly have an impact on any decision related to the future of the training program; however, there are other factors that may make it impossible to come to a decision solely on the basis of the confirmative evaluation results: unanticipated budgetary restraints; new regulatory or certification requirements; political or ethical issues; a merger, acquisition, or joint venture; and so on.

Improve Performance

When you peel away the layers, you find that decision-making stakeholders are really focused on improving performance. Although their decisions strongly affect the future of the training program, their original, basic information needs are aimed at improving the performance of individuals, work groups or business groups, external groups such as customers and suppliers, the organization as a whole, and even the global community within which the organization functions.

Decision makers who become the stakeholders for the confirmative evaluation of a training program carry their improvement efforts back to the

Table 7.1. Decision, Decisions, Decisions.

Continuous Improvement Evaluation Outcome	Decision Options	
	If	Then
Continuing competence of the learner	Level of competency meets standards	☐ Maintain the program
	Level of competency does not meet standards	☐ Revise the program
	New context requires new standards	☐ Revise the program ☐ Discard the program ☐ Replace the program
Continuing effectiveness of training program design	Effective	☐ Maintain the program
	Somewhat effective	☐ Revise the program
	Not effective	☐ Discard the program ☐ Replace the program
Continuous performance or quality improvement of individual, business group, or organization	Program ongoing and effective	☐ Maintain the program
	Program ongoing and not effective	☐ Revise the program ☐ Discard the program ☐ Replace the program
	Program one-time or short-term	☐ Maintain the program ☐ Revise (increase program life cycle)

Table based on Van Tiem, D. M., Moseley, J. L., and Dessinger, J. C. *Fundamentals of Performance Technology: A Guide to Improving People, Process, and Performance.* © 2000 International Society for Performance Improvement, pp. 176–177.

office, the line, or the boardroom. If goals and objectives are properly aligned, then a well-designed training program produces well-trained individuals who perform at a level of excellence that positively increases the performance level of their work group or business group, which in turn has a positive impact on the organization and brings value to both the organization and the global community. Sometimes training is enough; sometimes, more or different performance interventions are required, and the well-informed practitioner steers the decision makers beyond training and development to financial, personal development, work redesign, or other noninstructional performance improvement interventions (Van Tiem, Moseley, and Dessinger, 2001).

Another way to improve performance is to manage the problem of transferring knowledge and skill from the training program to the job. Hodges (2002) suggests that "the evaluator can be the *gatekeeper* for transfer by ensuring the program task force (stakeholders, managers, designers, implementers, and sometimes trainers and participants) addresses the issues in the planning phases of the program. . . . to prevent them from becoming barriers" (pp. 107–108).

Improve Quality

Decision makers should also focus on improving quality, whether it is the quality of the training program; of the organization's processes, products, or services; or of the evaluation itself. Continuous quality improvement (CQI)—also known as total quality management (TQM) in the manufacturing environment—focuses on improving processes for delivering products or services and is central to the purpose of confirmative evaluation. Many of the confirmative evaluation concepts presented in this book are elements of CQI:

- Focus on all stakeholder and customer needs.

- Ensure top-level management commitment and participation.

- Use a team or collaborative approach to planning, implementation, and follow-up.

- Monitor programs and processes to drive and validate performance improvement.

- Actively implement quality improvement that is based on stakeholder and customer needs.

How can the evaluation, training, or HPT practitioner use the CQI framework to improve performance? It's really a matter of educating, emphasizing, getting involved, and encouraging:

- *Educate* the organization about the inputs, process, outputs, and outcomes of confirmative evaluation.

- *Emphasize* how useful they are for planning, implementing, and evaluating continuous improvement.

- *Get involved* with existing CQI (or TQM) initiatives within your organization.

- *Encourage* the quality managers and team members to use your expertise in confirmative evaluation (and training or HPT) to their advantage and that of the organization.

Improve the Evaluation Process

Practitioners must be willing to take the risk of validating their work, especially when that work is evaluation. One way to minimize the personal risk and maximize the results is to hire an external evaluator to perform a meta evaluation. Meta evaluation not only validates the results of the confirmative evaluation but also judges the merit and worth of the confirmative evaluation inputs, process, outputs, and outcomes. Type one meta evaluation performs the validation concurrently with the various evaluation activities; type two meta evaluation looks back at the evaluation after it is completed.

Assume the Role

So far, we have suggested traditional roles of the practitioner during confirmative evaluation of a training program: planner, data collector, data analyst, interpreter, report writer, and communicator. Patton (1997) and Hodges (2002), among others, would broaden the role of the twenty-first-century evaluation, training, or HPT practitioner to include more active involvement in postevaluation activities. We also see the practitioner as a partner in continuous improvement, actively working with decision makers and offering support and expertise as needed to facilitate, monitor, and validate continuous improvement activities.

The Toolbox at the end of this chapter refers you to a utilization enhancement checklist of *traditional* roles and responsibilities for an evaluator or training consultant. Here are some *nontraditional* suggestions for the twenty-first-century practitioner who does not want his or her role to be limited to *plan-do-analyze:*

- Participate in existing continuous improvement initiatives; become known as a change agent.

- Recommend continuous improvement efforts that are based on confirmative evaluation outcomes.

- Know how to use instructional and performance technology or quality techniques and tools to solve performance problems and improve performance; share your expertise.

- Facilitate the processes that lead to change; be a change agent.

- Monitor and document the follow-up actions agreed on by the stakeholders during confirmative evaluation planning activities.

- Help decision makers focus on the benefits of improved performance, recognize and overcome current barriers to improved performance, and predict future barriers on the basis of confirmative evaluation results.

The involvement of the practitioner in continuous improvement activities should be limited only by individual knowledge, expertise, and willingness to seek and accept the challenge.

Accept the Challenge

The major challenges to the evaluation, training, or HPT practitioner during the *improve* phase arise from the very nature of performance and quality improvement efforts. These are some predictable challenges:

- Determine levels of accountability for continuous improvement.

- Maintain stakeholder commitment to continuous improvement.

- Establish credibility as a decision-making partner.

- Overcome the tendency toward inertia when confirmative evaluation outcomes are positive.

- Keep focused on utilization throughout the confirmative evaluation process and beyond.

- Become a change agent.

- Take risks.

Accept Accountability for Continuous Improvement

We have examined traditional (and potential or nontraditional) roles and responsibilities of the practitioner, and we have discussed the fact that there is disagreement in the field regarding whether the practitioner should participate in continuous improvement activities beyond the confirmative evaluation final report. Is the training or HPT practitioner accountable for the performance of the business or work group, individual, or organization after participants complete the training program? Is *improve* really a part of the confirmative evaluation process? If so, should the practitioner play a significant role in any continuous improvement initiative that results from the outcomes of the confirmative evaluation?

Back in 1989, Jackson suggested to training and development professionals that "you do not have the responsibility for ensuring that the training you do yields results operationally and organizationally (although the finger will probably point at you if your training is of no value to the line)" (pp. 52–53). More recently, Moseley and Solomon (1997, p. 14) discussed "heightened awareness of accountability" and Esque (2001, p. 11) suggests that training and HPT practitioners must be willing to assume "accountability for measurable contributions to the bottom line." Trends such as those listed in Chapter Nine of this book also suggest that the training or HPT practitioner, and even the evaluator, may need to take an active role in making sure that *improve* is an integral, vital, continuing part of the confirmative evaluation process as well as of the entire training and development function. As the training and development professional evolves into an HPT practitioner, his or her role during confirmative evaluation also becomes much broader and more inclusive, and there is increasing emphasis on professional accountability.

Maintain Stakeholder Commitment

During the *plan* phase of the confirmative evaluation process (see Chapter Three), the practitioner completed the evaluability assessment process by asking the stakeholders to create and commit to using the outcomes of the confirmative evaluation to improve performance or quality. The challenge to maintain stakeholder commitment to action continues throughout the confirmative evaluation process: "Evaluations should be planned, conducted, and reported in ways that encourage follow-through by stakeholders, so that the likelihood that the evaluation will be used is increased" (The Joint Committee on Standards for Educational Evaluation, 1994, pp. 442–443).

As new stakeholders replace original stakeholders or are added to the list of people who have a vested interest in the outcomes of the confirmative evaluation, the practitioner should assess their information needs, adjust the intended confirmative evaluation outcomes if necessary, and encourage the new stakeholders to create and commit to an action plan. In addition, the practitioner should communicate with the stakeholders throughout the confirmative evaluation process.

Establish Credibility as a Partner

One potential role of the practitioner is to partner with the stakeholders who have the power to make operational, administrative, management, or marketing decisions that affect the entire organization (and even the global marketplace). The practitioner may offer encouragement, experience, expertise, and other support to enable and monitor the decision-making process and keep it focused on the intended outcomes of the confirmative evaluation.

The challenge is to establish credibility as a decision-making partner. The practitioner should be perceived as a professional who has the knowledge, expertise, and experience to:

- Help decision makers clarify their decision options prior to developing action plans for continuous improvement

- Verify that the intended evaluation outcomes and confirmative evaluation questions support decision making

- Facilitate evaluation, performance improvement, and change processes

- Stay focused on decision-making options during data collection, analysis, and interpretation

- Recommend continuous improvement options that are based on confirmative evaluation outcomes as well as the structure, climate, and culture of the organization

- Prepare a final report that supports decision making and helps the decision makers justify their decisions, especially if the choices influence the entire organization or the global community

Credibility is a perception that must be developed and nurtured. Credentials help build credibility—for example, an academic degree or professional certification in instructional or performance technology, or a professional reference from a past confirmative evaluation or performance improvement project. Being visible, knowledgeable, and willing to share knowledge and expertise also helps build credibility.

Overcome Inertia from Positive Evaluations

When intended confirmative evaluation outcomes are positive, especially if they are highly positive, there is often a tendency to say, "If the program is so efficient, effective, high-impact, or valuable, why improve it?" or "Now that we know the outcomes are good, we don't need to continue evaluating this training program." The practitioner can overcome this inertia by making it clear in the final report that there is always room for improvement; good is fine, but better is better, and best is best. Even if the level of performance now meets performance standards, or the training or learning intervention is measurably effective over time, there is always the option to exceed the standards or raise the bar, increase effectiveness, and delight and dazzle the customer. At the very least, the evaluation, training, or HPT practitioner should encourage the stakeholders and the organization to recycle the full-scope evaluation plan throughout the life of the training program.

Maintain Focus on Utilization

The challenge begins in the plan phase, when the utilization-focused practitioner must validate that the information needs of the stakeholders are relevant and useful and that the true decision makers are included in and committed to the confirmative evaluation process. During the *do* phase, the challenge is to collect credible and useful data that may be used during the *improve* phase. Patton (1997) presents these "political maxims" to help utilization-focused evaluators meet the challenge of use:

- Not all information is useful.

- Not all people are information users.

- Information targeted at use is more likely to hit the target.

- Only credible information is ultimately powerful (pp. 350–351).

Become a Change Agent

Confirmative evaluation's commitment to continuous improvement centers it in the vortex of major organizational change. The HPT practitioner assumes the role of a change agent and becomes responsible for "producing independent, unbiased, empirical evidence of the operations and performance of organizational entities" that can drive effective change (Sonnichsen, 1994, p. 537). To fulfill the roles and responsibilities of change agent, the practitioner must make recommendations for change that are based not only on reliable and valid data (data that consistently measure what they say they will measure) but also on a thorough knowledge and understanding of the organization's mission, culture, climate, and values.

Take Risks

Evaluators, training or HPT practitioners, and others who work on a confirmative evaluation project are often called on to take risks. These risks arise from (among other sources) the need to make decisions, finalize negotiations, fulfill promises, and blend collaborative inputs. Risk taking has many faces. You may recognize the face of risk in any number of situations:

- Sticking out your neck for someone or something you strongly believe in

- Taking an educated risk, according to what you have learned from professional sources

- Believing in yourself and your own capabilities

- Expecting and maintaining high standards for yourself and others

- Adapting to a change in the culture of an organization

- Adjusting to the uncertainties of the business world

- Building alternative actions into the confirmative evaluation plan and being courageous enough to switch from Plan A to Plan B

- Saying what you believe and standing behind your beliefs

- Appreciating competition

- Valuing collaboration with stakeholders and sponsors

- Recommending proactive solutions to address negative confirmative evaluation results

- Seeking minority opinions when it is not politic to do so

- Valuing how diversity affects the inputs, process, outputs, and outcomes of confirmative evaluation

- Maintaining professional and personal ethics during the confirmative evaluation process

Behold the turtle, making no progress without sticking its neck out!

Alignment: The Last Word

Training is a performance improvement intervention. It has an effect on the behavior of the individual, group, business, organization, and global community within which the organization operates. Proper use of ADDI/E (See Chapter One) or a similar systematic model for instructional design ensures that the intended performance outcomes of the training program are aligned with the intended outcomes of the program's stakeholders, which in turn are aligned with organizational mission, values, and goal. Alignment is important as a precursor for the success of all phases of confirmative evaluation. It is especially important for the success of the *improve* phase because alignment validates the results of the confirmative evaluation and forms the foundation for continuous improvement. So, when and how does the practitioner test for alignment? The answer is, throughout the confirmative evaluation process.

Jackson (1989) suggests a trickle-down approach to *targeted evaluation*. He believes that if training "objectives with definite targets are set out beforehand [and] if they are achieved, we can assume that our intervention has had the desired effect; it is thus validated" (p. 105). We take this analogy a step further by suggesting that validation also requires action: (1) conscious, deliberate alignment of the targets (intended confirmative evaluation outcomes) with the organization's mission, values, and culture prior to conducting the confirmative evaluation; and (2) conscious, deliberate maintenance of the alignment throughout the confirmative evaluation process.

PST 7.1 is an action guide to help the practitioner determine whether organizational goals and objectives, stakeholder information needs, and confirmative evaluation outcomes are aligned and will support action for continuous improvement.

PST 7.1. Testing Alignment to Build a Foundation for Continuous Improvement.

Purpose: To validate that action for continuous improvement is based on the alignment of organizational goals and objectives, stakeholder information needs, and intended confirmative evaluation outcomes.

Directions: Use the outputs of steps one through three to write the confirmative evaluation plan. Review the outputs of steps one through three regularly to make sure they still reflect current conditions. Revise the confirmative evaluation plan if needed.

Note: For the purpose of this book, we are assuming that training is selected in step three as the appropriate performance intervention to ensure that operational needs are met.

Steps to Testing for Alignment	Potential Output	Timing
1. **Review** what the organization is trying to achieve; clarify ideas and strategy if necessary.	• Organization mission and value statement • List of strategic goals and objectives	*Plan* phase
2. **Discover** the operational means the organization is using to achieve its stated objectives.	• Analysis of business unit or work group operational plans • Analysis of results from interviews, surveys, group activities	*Plan* phase
3. **Assess** what must be done to ensure that operational needs are met.	• Negotiated list of training needs from all stakeholders • List of needs generated by management	*Plan* phase
4. **Focus** on designing a training program that aligns with operational needs.	• Training program plan • Evaluation plan • Interim reports	*Plan* phase, and just prior to the *do* phase
5. **Measure** the achievements of the training program to determine the degree to which the program has met the operational needs (which met the organizational needs, which met the needs of the global community).	• Formative and summative evaluation reports • Confirmative evaluation report • Recommendations for results-based action	*Do* and *analyze* phases
6. **Take action** to improve performance; perform a reality check (steps one through three) regularly.	• Stakeholder action plans • Progress reports • Alignment-based revisions as needed	*Improve* phase

SUMMARY: LESSONS LEARNED IN CHAPTER SEVEN

1. The role of the evaluation, training, or HPT practitioner during the *improve* phase of confirmative evaluation is largely dependent on the structure, climate, and culture of the organization.

2. The roles of the practitioner during the *improve* phase of confirmative evaluation may include decision-making partner, change agent, and risk taker, and each role involves issues of credibility and accountability.

3. The *improve* phase focuses on the training program, the organization (individuals, groups, businesses), and the confirmative evaluation itself.

4. Meta evaluation is risky business, but it helps establish the credibility and accountability of the confirmative evaluation inputs, process, outputs, and outcomes and of the practitioner.

5. Personal lessons learned:

_____

_____

_____

_____

_____

_____

_____

_____

_____

NEXT STEPS

The last part of this book contains a case study and meta evaluation of a confirmative evaluation and discusses challenges, old and new, that have an impact on evaluation in general and confirmative evaluation in particular. You will conduct a self-assessment to determine whether you possess the characteristics of a stellar confirmative evaluator.

TOOLBOX FOR UTILIZATION-FOCUSED EVALUATORS

These professional resources present in-depth discussion and practical information on using evaluation results to improve performance and quality. Although the resources focus on utilization, they offer practical ways to apply the theory and practice of utilization-focused evaluation to confirmative evaluation.

Professional Books

Patton, M. Q. *Utilization Focused Evaluation: The New Century Text* (3rd ed.). Thousand Oaks, Calif.: Sage, 1997. (Presents the challenges, mandates, realities, and practicalities of implementing utilization-focused evaluation.)

Rothwell, W. J. *Beyond Training and Development: State of the Art Strategies for Enhancing Human Performance.* New York: AMACOM, 1996. (Views the training or HPT practitioner as a partner in performance improvement.)

Van Tiem, D. M., Moseley, J. L., and Dessinger, J. C. *Performance Improvement Interventions: Enhancing People, Processes, and Organizations Through Performance Technology.* Silver Spring, Md.: International Society for Performance Improvement, 2001. (Introduces a variety of performance improvement interventions other than training and gives practical advice on how to select and implement the most appropriate intervention.)

Self-Assessment

"Utilization Enhancement Checklist." In L. A. Braskamp and R. A. Brown (eds.), *New Directions for Program Evaluation: Utilization of Evaluative Information.* San Francisco: Jossey-Bass, 1980. (Fifty-item checklist on self-analysis, understanding the organizational context, planning the evaluation, the evaluation process, and communication.)

Web-Based Resource

The Program Evaluations Metaevaluation Checklist is available at www.wmich.edu/evalctr/checklists

PART 3

Lessons from Oz

Think the current state of confirmative evaluation is a challenge? It will take more than ruby slippers and clicking your heels to envision and plan for a future of new and exciting possibilities.

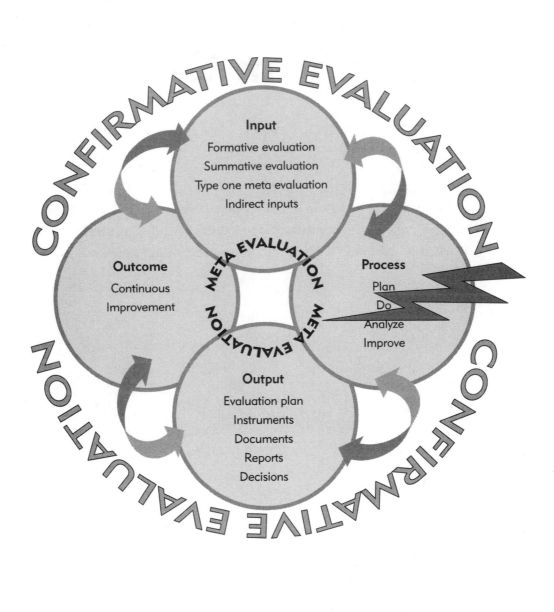

8

Case Study: Lions and Tigers and Bears, Oh My!

WHEN DOROTHY and her friends started off for the Emerald City, they were afraid of the lions and tigers and bears they assumed were out there waiting to keep them from reaching Oz. If Dorothy and friends had been evaluation, training, or HPT practitioners following the yellow brick road through the development and implementation of a training program, they would have known what was "out there" before they began the journey and conducted a full-scope evaluation before, during, and after. Formative and summative evaluation strategies would have taken care of any lions or tigers or bears they met along the way, confirmative evaluation would have verified that they had reached Oz, and meta evaluation would have helped assure them that the whole journey was *real*.

This chapter presents a confirmative evaluation case study that is part fact and part fiction—and replete with lions and tigers and bears (real and imagined). The reactive confirmative evaluation is quite typical of the manner in which people in today's organizations understand and execute the confirmative process. First, we present the case study; then we conduct a meta evaluation of the case study to complete the confirmative evaluation process.

After reading this chapter, you will be able to:

1. Appreciate the complexity of the confirmative evaluation process, especially at the focusing and data-gathering phases

2. Identify some of the lions and tigers and bears that may confront real-world confirmative evaluation efforts

3. Review a meta evaluation of a case study

4. Recognize the benefits of full-scope evaluation

The Case Study

The Emerald City Zoo is a typical large, nonprofit, metropolitan zoo. Munchkins come from all over Oz to enjoy the animal displays and other activities at the zoo, and to volunteer as docents. This is their story—and the story of the zoo's stakeholders, who take their responsibility for continuous improvement at the Emerald City Zoo very, very seriously.

Program Overview

The Emerald City Zoo has an extensive training program for all munchkins who want to become docents or volunteer elsewhere in the zoo. All prospective volunteers must complete three basic steps prior to entering a specific volunteer training program:

• Attend a prospective volunteer orientation session. Every month, prospective volunteers are introduced to the volunteer opportunities offered at the zoo (special events volunteer, office aide, gallery guide, docent). Representatives from each of these programs describe the job, typical working conditions, and annual requirements.

• Meet with a volunteer services staff member for an interview and discussion of placement.

- Attend a general orientation session. This three-hour training class is designed to give a consistent and thorough overview of the Emerald City Zoo and its safety procedures.

At this point, munchkins who aspire to become docents go into the Docent Training Program. The thirteen-week program was developed by the zoo's training staff with input from volunteer services staff and docents. After the program was developed, piloted, and revised, training workshops were offered to instruct experienced docents on how to conduct the training.

Goal. The goal of the Docent Training Program is to present docent trainees with basic zoology background information, familiarization with the Emerald City Zoo and its initiatives, and basic interpretive skills to effectively communicate with diverse audiences. Training materials support the program goals. Trainees receive a list of course objectives and a checklist of necessary activities that they need to perform to successfully complete the course. They also receive a training manual, which contains an assortment of resources (class outlines, animal fact sheets, and copies of the animal exhibit graphics).

Instructional Strategies. Nine of the training sessions occur in a classroom at the Emerald City Zoo. Since the zoo itself is a living classroom, the other four training sessions occur within the zoo grounds. Students are seated at tables so that they can interact with others during the class. Trainers use a variety of instructional strategies to teach basic zoological concepts and interpretive skills.

In general, a portion of the class consists of formal lecture presentation and class discussion. Instructors use slides and other visual aids to illustrate important concepts. Biofacts on skulls, feathers, furs, and models are used for hands-on experiences. The trainees also receive homework and reading assignments.

Since the zoo's training department promotes inquiry learning, the trainers model questioning techniques for trainees. A second portion of the class is devoted to developing and enhancing interpretive skills through a variety of activities, such as role playing real-life zoo situations, curator talks, walking tours, videotape reviews, auditing tours, shadowing exhibit interpretations, games such as Mammal Jeopardy, and so forth.

Mentoring, Coaching, and Feedback. Trainees are assigned a munchkin mentor. Mentors are experienced docents who attend most class sessions and offer insight drawn from their experience. Mentors work with small groups and are able to give the students tips and advice based on their accumulated experiences. In addition to attending thirteen weekly training sessions, docent trainees are expected to audit two tours conducted by an experienced docent and practice at two animal interpretation shifts with their mentor.

Training staff members interact with docents daily to ensure that they are comfortable in their job and are receiving any necessary feedback. There are class quizzes; participants must score 85 percent or higher on two exams, a written zoology test, and an interpretive walking tour test.

Outcomes. After successfully completing the Docent Training Program, the munchkins begin their career as an active docent. Docent activities include:

- Scheduling time for volunteering
- Leading groups of ten individuals of all ages
- Interpreting animal exhibits
- Staffing zoo exhibits at community events and fairs and interacting with visitors
- Delivering presentations at off-site locations

Active docents must also maintain records of their activities at the zoo, complete a minimum of seventy-five education hours during the calendar year, and complete an annual recertification event. This event changes from year to year according to needs. Throughout the year, volunteer auditors check docent records, and a letter is sent out to contact individuals who lack the required number of service hours. In addition to regular docent activities, the volunteer services office or the training department develops enrichment events to further educate and enhance the docents' efficiency and satisfaction. Examples of enrichment events are monthly meetings with updates from the animal curators and continuing education classes.

Rewards and Recognition. Docent hours are tallied monthly and summarized at the end of the year. Individual pins are awarded every April to docents who reach specific benchmarks (for example, 100 tours, 100 exhibit interpretation shifts, 150 outreach presentations, and so forth). All zoo volunteers, including docents, who have contributed more than twenty hours in a year are invited to attend the Volunteer Recognition Ball.

Trigger Event

One day, the Wizard of Oz, who serves as chair of the Emerald City Zoo Advisory Council, calls the zoo's director and says, "The advisory council would like to know whether the munchkins who volunteer as docents like the current docent training program. Does it make them good docents?"

The zoo's director talks to the training director; the training director talks to the volunteer services director; the training staff meet with the volunteer services staff and representatives from the Docents Association; and three months and several meetings later the training director delivers a proposal to the advisory council:

On the basis of stakeholder input, the training department has decided to conduct a confirmative evaluation of the Docent Training Program to determine whether the program is effective and has a positive impact on the docents. The evaluation will answer four questions:

1. Did the docents accomplish the training program objectives for effective performance as a docent?
2. How did the trainees feel about the content of the training program?
3. Were the trainees satisfied with the instructor's delivery?
4. Were the trainees satisfied with the training program?

The advisory council says, "This seems to meet our needs just fine."

Stakeholder Input

The stakeholders who provide the input are a diverse group with equally diverse needs. They include internal stakeholders such as docents and zoo staff and external stakeholders such as visitors, funding agencies, and others. Training department staff conduct informal individual and group interviews to gather most of the information.

Docents. More than 100 munchkins volunteer as docents at the zoo. The mission of the docent volunteers is to act as *front-line* educators, generate interest and enthusiasm about animals and the environment, and motivate visitors to help preserve nature. Docents perform a variety of jobs, among them leading tours, interacting with visitors at animal exhibits, and delivering presentations in the community. Representatives from the Docent Association meet monthly with zoo staff from volunteer services and the training department to help develop and maintain docent recruitment, training, retention, and recognition programs.

Docents come from a variety of backgrounds—housewives, plumbers, dentists, and teachers, to mention just a few. More than half are retired from a formal career. Most docents have had at least two to four years of college; however, they vary significantly in their background knowledge of zoology. Some docents may have a degree in the field; others may not have any formal exposure, with the possible exception of high school. Docents are usually self-motivated to learn more about animals and the zoo, and they tend to be good readers. Docents also tend to have outgoing personalities and a desire to interact with others. An informal survey of both prospective and active docents indicates that despite their wide variety of backgrounds, docents expect that the Docent Training Program will help them function as competent and confident docents and enjoy their volunteer experience at the Emerald City Zoo.

Staff. Internal stakeholders include the zoo's administration and administrative staff, volunteer services, and the training department. The administrative staff does not deal directly with the docents; however, they need to verify that the training program produces docents who are positive and competent ambassadors of the zoo.

Volunteer services is responsible for recruiting prospective zoo volunteers, introducing them to various volunteer opportunities at the zoo, and retaining volunteers. Volunteer services also hosts update meetings to share with all new volunteers information on the zoo and emergency preparedness, tabulates and documents volunteer hours, and is responsible for the annual Volunteer Recognition Ball. Volunteer services also works with the training staff to develop and maintain the training program. The volunteer services staff needs input to help them build a strong volunteer program by successfully recruiting and retaining a group of diverse docents.

The training department consists of the zoo curator, the associate curator of education, and two education assistants. The training department is responsible for all the Emerald City Zoo's education and training programs, including those for zoo administration, staff, visitors, volunteers, and the community of Oz. In turn, the training department relies on docents to educate zoo visitors, participate in community outreach programs, and coach novice docents. The training department needs to know whether the training program meets its performance objectives and whether the trainees like the program.

External Stakeholders. External stakeholders include parents, children, school personnel, city officials, zoo personnel, animal activists, zoo advocates, taxpayers in general, and other interested zoo patrons who share an interest in and concern for the general well-being of animals and their survival in natural, humane settings. External stakeholders in general rely on the docents to positively influence the zoo experience for all visitors and encourage the visitors to return to the zoo regularly. Taxpayers and granting organizations who help fund the zoo also rely on the munchkin docents for good return on investment by competently, effectively, and efficiently implementing their job activities.

Confirmative Evaluation Activities

An evaluation team from the training department conducts the confirmative evaluation. The activities include benchmarking other zoos, collecting and analyzing data, and communicating the results to the advisory council.

Benchmarking. The evaluation team selects a well-known zoo in their sister city in Kansas, as well as other zoos that are comparable in size to the Emerald City Zoo. Team members communicate with zoo officials and use their knowledge and expertise to help the team focus the confirmative evaluation. As a result of the benchmarking activities, the evaluation team looks at four foci for evaluating the effectiveness of the Docent Training Program:

1. Training objectives

2. Student progress

3. Training content

4. Docent satisfaction

Given the current situation at the Emerald City Zoo (existing formative and summative evaluation activities, time, resources), the evaluation team decides to remain focused on the training objectives and docent satisfaction with the training program (content, instructor delivery, and overall satisfaction) as the basis for confirming the effectiveness of the Docent Training Program.

Data Collection. The evaluation team then identifies multiple potential data sources for collecting data to answer the confirmative evaluation questions: instructor surveys, reflective surveys, class content quizzes, final written exam scores, final walking-tour rating results, and the report from an outside vendor's summative evaluation of one of the exhibits.

Instructor Surveys. Docent trainees traditionally critique the instructor's delivery of each training session content. Surveys are collected before trainees leave the class and are given to the instructor.

Reflective Surveys. Docent trainees complete this survey after they leave a session. The survey allows the trainees to reflect on their own feelings about the lesson and also helps the instructor identify topics in which students need help.

Quizzes. Docent trainees take several quizzes throughout the course, and there is a written examination at the completion of the thirteen-week training program. The essay exam tests key zoological concepts presented throughout the course. The trainees cannot use books or notes to write this exam.

Walking Tour. After completing the written exam, docent trainees shadow seasoned docents as they lead walking tours of the zoo. After two shadowing events, each docent trainee conducts two stationary tours with the aid of his or her mentor, to gauge the trainee's interpretive and interpersonal skills. Trainees are given precisely defined criteria in advance. Groups of four or five trainees tour the zoo with education staff to make their presentations. The staff rates the students on these criteria: age appropriateness of content and delivery, audience involvement through questioning, use of teachable moments, knowledge of information and facts, use of visual aids such as graphics and signage, staying topic-focused, adherence to time constraints, eye contact, voice clarity, and effective use of transition time between animal exhibits.

Summative Evaluation. An external evaluator is conducting a summative evaluation of the new tiger exhibit. The plan includes an evaluation of docent effectiveness from the perspective of zoo patrons.

Docent Survey. The training department evaluation team has created a docent survey to measure docent satisfaction with the training program.

Data Analysis Interpretation and Recommendations. Usable, quantitative data from the instructor and reflective surveys, the class content quizzes, the essay tests, and the walking tour rating forms are reviewed by the trainers and then returned to the docents for their use as a continuous improvement feedback mechanism. The only existing data are a pass-fail designation in individual trainee records for the final essay exam and the walking tour. However, the student records are not coded to indicate who needs to retake the essay exam or the walking tour in order to pass the course, and only the most recent student records are computerized. Trainers estimate that "60–75 percent of the trainees pass the course the first time."

The evaluation team is also unable to collect data from the summative evaluation of the tiger exhibit. The vendor delivers the results in the form of a PowerPoint presentation during a meeting at the wizard's palace. There are technical problems with the wizard's equipment, and the data are lost. The vendor has not kept a backup copy.

The evaluation team is able to pilot the Docent Satisfaction Survey with fifteen recent graduates of the training program. The team plans to tabulate and graph the quantitative data and summarize the qualitative data in narrative form; however, at this point the entire zoo staff becomes involved in the major spring fundraiser and work on the confirmative evaluation is tabled. The evaluation team does, though, issue an interim memo to the advisory council that is based on a review of the Docent Satisfaction Survey pilot results, and the problems that have occurred during data collection. The team makes four recommendations:

1. Provide additional support to docents to help lessen their reported anxiety level over the vast amount of information they need to learn and interpret.

2. Measure docent anxiety level throughout the training program, graph the results, and show how expert docents handle the information load as they progress through the training.

3. Examine how the Emerald City Zoo, in concert with the community at large, can further recognize the tremendous efforts of the volunteer docents.

4. Document and archive all evaluation records so that future evaluation teams can review data generated from previous evaluations.

Table 8.1 summarizes the Docent Training Program confirmative evaluation.

Table 8.1. Summary of Docent Training Program Confirmative Evaluation.

Evaluation Questions	Data Sources	Analysis and Interpretation of Results	Recommendations
1. Did the trainees accomplish the training program objectives?	• Quiz results • Final examination results • Summative evaluation results • Final walking tour results	No data available	• Tabulate results from quizzes and final exams • Archive data and results from quizzes and final exams • Reconstruct data from summative evaluation
2. How did the trainees feel about the content of the training program?	• Reflective survey results • Pilot docent satisfaction survey	• Data not available from reflective survey • Pilot survey results not reported, analyzed, or interpreted	• Provide additional support to docents to help lessen their anxiety level over the vast amount of information they need to learn and interpret
3. Were the trainees satisfied with the instructors' delivery?	• Instructor survey results • Pilot docent satisfaction survey	• Data not available from instructor survey • Results from pilot survey not reported, analyzed, or interpreted	• Archive survey data
4. Were the trainees satisfied with the training program?	• Instructor survey results • Reflective survey results • Pilot docent satisfaction survey	• Data not available from instructor or reflective surveys • Pilot survey results not reported, analyzed, or interpreted	• Examine how the zoo and the community can further recognize the tremendous efforts of the docents

Meta Evaluation

Meta evaluation—evaluating the evaluation itself—is at the heart of the Confirmative Evaluation Model. Conducting a meta evaluation is the final step in any confirmative evaluation process (including the one used here in our case study). In Chapter One and Table 1.1, we addressed the definition and scope of meta evaluation. It completes the full-scope evaluation landscape. It is a quality control process that provides feedback on the reliability and validity of the evaluation processes, products, and results.

The Joint Committee on Standards for Educational Evaluation (1994) issued and revised a set of thirty standards for quality evaluation that apply to both education and training programs. The standards furnish a common language and a set of rules and guiding principles that serve as a basis for judging accountability and credibility. They address issues such as utility, feasibility, propriety, and accuracy and are helpful for any practitioner who conducts a meta evaluation of a confirmative evaluation.

The zoo case study illustrates the potential usefulness of confirmative evaluation outcomes in guiding decision making—for example, the potential for using evaluation data to improve docent training and retention. It also illustrates how important it is to train HPT or training practitioners to conduct confirmative evaluation using a sound systematic and systemic process, and how it is equally important to inform the decision makers about the process and potential of confirmative evaluation.

Table 8.2 summarizes the strengths and weaknesses of the Docent Training Program confirmative evaluation. The major strength of the confirmative evaluation is that it raises two major issues that affect program effectiveness: information overload and the critical need to document and archive evaluation data. The major limitation is the maximum disruption that occurs when the evaluation team attempts to collect the data vital to the success of the evaluation.

Table 8.2. Strengths and Limitations of Docent Training Program Confirmative Evaluation.

Strengths	Limitations
The Emerald City Zoo Advisory Council recognized the basic need to confirm the merit and worth of long-term training.	• The evaluation team needed to educate the advisory council regarding the resources required to perform an effective confirmative evaluation.
The evaluation team identified all the stakeholders and asked the right question: What do the individual stakeholder groups need to know about the zoo's docent program?	• The evaluation team did not suggest looking beyond immediate docent accomplishments and reaction to training.
Cooperation and collaboration efforts are stressed among the Emerald City Zoo staff and volunteers.	• The collaborators did not communicate about the availability of required evaluation data.
The stakeholders gathered information on effectiveness from the docents.	• The confirmative evaluation was limited to evaluating the effectiveness of the training program from the viewpoint of the docents. • There were no data on how zoo patrons (one of the major stakeholder groups) evaluate their interaction with trained docents.
The evaluation team identified potential data sources.	• The evaluation team did not determine whether the data were actually available to them. • It is impossible to conduct a meaningful confirmative evaluation if records and data are unavailable.
The evaluation team developed and piloted an instrument to collect data on docent reaction to the training.	• The survey addressed only docent satisfaction with content, delivery, and the overall program.
The pilot survey uncovered program weaknesses that can be addressed to improve performance.	• The pilot population did not include input from trainees who left the program or docents who left the zoo. • The evaluation team did not report any positive results from the pilot.
The evaluation team issued an interim report once work on the confirmative evaluation was halted.	• The evaluation team made recommendations based on the responses from a small, nonrandomized sampling of the population. • The report did not include the pass-fail estimates reported by the trainers or the problems with data collection.

Final Thoughts

In the preceding chapter we urged you to "Behold the turtle, making no progress without sticking its neck out!" If we are sincerely committed to the confirmative evaluation process, we must take appropriate risks to make it happen and report our results whether they are positive or negative. The evaluation team members were not trained as evaluators, but essentially they stuck their necks out, followed the basic confirmative evaluation process we have presented in this book, and planned a confirmative evaluation according to what they believed was the best-case scenario given the current constraints at the zoo. They took a risk, and hopefully that will be recognized in the future when the dust settles on fundraising and the turtle is once more on the move toward continuous improvement.

SUMMARY: LESSONS LEARNED IN CHAPTER EIGHT

Before continuing to the final chapter, take a few minutes to review some lessons learned here:

1. Reactive planning is real; proactive planning is ideal.

2. It is useful to document and archive formative and summative evaluation data—just in case.

3. Behold the turtle!

4. Personal lessons learned:

_____

_____

_____

_____

_____

_____

NEXT STEPS

In the final chapter, we follow Dorothy and her friends as they prepare to leave the land of Oz.

9

Conclusion: We're Not in Oz Anymore

J UST AS DOROTHY JOURNEYS back from the land of Oz only to find a new landscape, evaluation, training, and HPT practitioners find a new landscape every time they embark on a confirmative evaluation journey. The landscape is different now from what it used to be. Today's landscape is cluttered with the latest three Rs (restructuring, reengineering, rightsizing) plus mergers, acquisitions, joint ventures, partnerships, reputation, networks and alliances, focusing and mobilizing organizations, valuing and leveraging cultural differences, innovation, technology, intellectual and social capital, and so on. An effective practitioner knows the landscape and works with the diverse audiences that color it. Evaluation, training, and HPT practitioners must learn about the landscape from the eyes of multiple audiences, from voices that share diverse opinions, and from unique perspectives that may, in fact, be contrary to their own. They must situate themselves in the organization's culture and see the landscape for the first time.

This final chapter looks at future directions for supporting, maintaining, and valuing confirmative evaluation as an enabler in an organization's quest for continuous improvement. We want to emphasize that practitioners cannot click their sequined red slippers together to trigger continuous improvement; instead, they must actively facilitate change and take whatever risks are required to help improve performance and quality.

After reading this chapter you will be able to:

1. Identify trends that have an impact on the role of confirmative evaluation in training and development

2. Appreciate the complexity of the confirmative evaluation process

3. Appreciate the challenges imposed by confirmative evaluation

4. List some qualities of a stellar confirmative evaluator

5. Determine the qualities *you* possess that will make *you* a stellar confirmative evaluator

Issues That Challenge Confirmative Evaluators

There are still, though, a variety of issues that practitioners face in carrying out their confirmative evaluation activities. The issues may stem from one-time events or ongoing trends; they influence an organization's quest for continuous improvement, and they challenge the practitioner. Here are some of the challenging issues encountered before, during, and after confirmative evaluation:

- Growing respect for the confirmative evaluation process
- Need for a more sophisticated evaluation workforce
- Need to form partnerships with stakeholders
- Increase in evaluation-driven improvement and decision making
- Challenge of permanent change
- Commitment to advocacy evaluation
- Knowing the territory
- Confirmative evaluation as a quality kaleidoscope
- Emphasis on ethics and ethical standards

Growing Respect for the Confirmative Evaluation Process

Organizations are moving beyond measurement of reaction, learning, and even transfer; there is considered interest and need for measuring long-term training program effectiveness, efficiency, impact, and value. As the confirmative evaluation process continues to gain respect and enthusiasm from organizations, the evaluation, training, or HPT practitioner must go beyond formative and summative evaluation and learn to walk the talk of confirmative evaluation.

Need for a More Sophisticated Evaluation Workforce

The trend toward more and better evaluation practices may call for formally prepared training or HPT practitioners who possess the evaluation skills of a well-trained evaluator. In addition to stellar technical expertise, the evaluation, training, or HPT practitioner has to possess managerial and supervisory skills and conceptual skills that allow him or her to develop options. The wisdom of Solomon, the patience of Job, good practical sense, and credibility surely help in this area. In addition, the practitioner must mix sound ethical practices with a modicum of political savvy, and the ability to think critically. Finally, the preparation must be rounded out with on-the-job internships, fully sponsored and supported by organizations and mentored by seasoned evaluators.

Forming Partnerships with Stakeholders

Today's organizations face numerous challenges brought on by the three Rs. Organizations that once operated with the Lone Ranger spirit now are involved in partnerships with multiple stakeholders who have diverse needs and interests. Practitioners need to work with stakeholders by involving them early in the evaluation process, keeping them informed about major decisions and pivotal issues, and seeking their advice on multiple levels. This partnership buy-in goes beyond good business practice; it becomes the lifeblood of the evaluation process.

Evaluation-Driven Improvement and Decision Making

To promote evaluation as a tool for improvement, practitioners must be situated in the right place at the right time to effect organizational change. They need to be fully aware of how decisions are made in the organization; how data are gathered, stored, and assimilated; and where the lines of authority lie. In the words of Sonnichsen (1994), ". . . the evaluation approach can be structured to complement the decision-making process. . . . Evaluators can contribute . . . only if evaluation results come to the attention of the decision makers in a format congruent with other data available at the appropriate time" (pp. 535, 541).

The Challenge of Permanent Change

The only constant in life is permanent change. Institutions in the future will experience large-scale changes. Numerous challenges will spin off current and future change efforts: mergers, acquisitions, joint ventures, rightsizing, reengineering, restructuring, e-learning, quality standards, strategic planning, cultural dimensions, and others. Sonnichsen writes: "Change in organizations requires a confluence of ideas, timing, support of top management, an organizational tolerance for risk, and individuals prepared to confront uncertainty in order to examine alternative ways to conduct organization business" (1994, p. 536). The practitioner who commits to confirmative evaluation must become a master of change.

Commitment to Advocacy Evaluation

If we believe that confirmative evaluation will influence organizational change and bottom-line results, then the practitioner's practice of submitting the evaluation report and ending involvement will give way to *advocacy evaluation,* which ". . . blends independent, scientific evaluation practices with an evaluator change-agent perspective. . . . [It] is defined as the active involvement of both evaluators and their supervisors in the organizational process of discussion, approval, and implementation of recommendations" (Sonnichsen, 1994, pp. 541–542).

Evaluation reports, no matter how sophisticated and well written, cannot speak for themselves. They need champions and advocates who can report their recommendations and conclusions to senior management and other top-ranking officials. To be viewed as influential players in the corporate board-room, practitioners should assume the advocacy evaluation approach. They must be totally committed to the organization, have a solid understanding of the business of the organization and how it competes in the global market, and be objective in negotiations. Only then will practitioners be considered viable members of the organization's strategic planning team.

Knowing the Territory

In the Broadway musical *Music Man,* Prof. Harold Hill says, "You've got to know the territory." The evaluation, training, or HPT practitioner must learn the territory of the business world and how it influences performance. Identifying and understanding business drivers and barriers helps the professional frame appropriate questions during evaluability and planning; select useful tools and techniques in the *do* stage; and give direction and focus to the analysis, interpretation, and communicating activities of the *analyze* stage of confirmative evaluation. Knowing the territory and the context in which the organizational climate and culture flourish also helps to set the stage for meaningful, relevant, customer-driven improvements that are based on sound confirmative evaluation outcomes.

Confirmative Evaluation as a Quality Kaleidoscope

Quality assurance is continuous; it is vitally important if confirmative evaluation is to be sustained and maintained in an organization. Quality assurance is all about assessing the quality of products or services or both. The services provided during confirmative evaluation by evaluators, training professionals, data collectors, analysts, and others, and the confirmative evaluation outputs, reports, and other documents, should be carefully scrutinized for quality.

In addition to offering input for the confirmative evaluation, the services provided by the practitioner and others involved in the evaluation process should be reviewed periodically. External evaluators and people who possess technical evaluation skills and knowledge and who are unrelated to the evaluation project could make these oversight services available. They would review the contract and the resulting deliverables; the evaluability plan, including the purpose and scope of the confirmative evaluation; the logs maintained during the evaluation process; the project management details, including the beginning and ending dates; and whatever other pertinent information is available for addressing performance issues.

Quality assurance also involves determining the quality of the final report. Peers and staff members who are familiar with both confirmative evaluation and the training program should review the confirmative evaluation plan and compare it with the final report. They should look for consistency with the selected design, appropriate statistics for accuracy, and the relevance of analysis and interpretation findings. This type of quality assurance is actually a type of meta evaluation.

Emphasis on Ethics and Ethical Standards

Evaluation, training, and HPT practitioners, as well as the confirmative evaluation's sponsors and stakeholders, must always maintain high ethical standards for conducting the evaluation and accepting its recommendations and conclusions. The commitment to maintain standards is embodied in the Golden Rule: "Do unto others as you would have them do unto you." This rule respects the rights and interests of individuals and society, and it protects the integrity of the confirmative evaluation process. There are professionally written ethical standards that guide evaluation practice; they are found in business, industry, government, health care, education, and so forth. Evaluation standards that apply to education and training were also developed by The Joint Committee on Standards for Educational Evaluation (1994). Following professional, ethical standards helps confirmative evaluation planners and implementers maintain the ethical integrity of the confirmative evaluation process. By maintaining an ethical stance, the organization, its personnel, and its external contractors demonstrate corporate integrity and increase the effectiveness of its public relations activities.

Evaluation as an Emerging Discipline

Some authors and professional writers treat evaluation as a field of study. We believe that evaluation is fast becoming a distinct discipline, forging ahead with new insight and direction. Professionals are writing evaluation books. Monographs treating performance topics now contain discussions and whole chapters on evaluation. The federal government requires evaluation as a condition for securing grant dollars. The enhanced human performance technology (HPT) model from the International Society for Performance Improvement (ISPI) elaborates on evaluation in human performance settings (Van Tiem, Moseley, and Dessinger, 2000). Evaluation as a distinct discipline has four aspects:

- Epistemological dimensions: a distinct subject matter, a methodology, and paradigms that delineate what knowledge is relevant, what the boundaries of the field are, and what the core problems are

- Sociological dimensions: professional organizations that support evaluation practice and their unique roles, the discipline in academia, governmental, and societal support for the discipline, communication patterns among practitioners in evaluation, and so forth

- Historical dimensions: when, where, why, and how the discipline emerged, its evolutionary stages, key action centers that support the discipline, and the impact the discipline of evaluation has on society

- Bibliographical dimensions: quantity of evaluation literature; its complexity and diversification; its chief organs of dissemination; how well the discipline is equipped with bibliographic and reference tools that embody, organize, package, and retrieve vital information and core knowledge pertinent to the discipline (M. Keresztesi, personal communication, Fall 1976).

Within evaluation, new areas are constantly being identified. This is especially true of confirmative evaluation. The term was first coined in 1978, and it is now worthy of consideration as a fully developed partner with its formative, summative, and meta evaluation siblings. As organizations struggle to maintain their corporate image and bottom-line results, and as they define their global presence and need for improving customer service by trying harder, empirical research and solid practice will further define the discipline of confirmative evaluation.

Improving the Process

Many opportunities exist for improving the confirmative evaluation process and for making it a permanent part of evaluation practice. Here are some suggestions for improvement:

- The discipline lacks empirical research in confirmative evaluation. New research studies must focus on application in practice.
- The literature on confirmative evaluation desperately needs well-written case studies reporting successes and failures. All professionals can learn if they are able to grasp what works and what does not work.
- Practitioners must take educated risks and remember the turtle (it makes no progress unless its neck is out).
- Practitioners need to develop a corporate-quality mind-set that permeates everything they do in confirmative evaluation; continuous quality improvement of products and services is required.
- The discipline needs practitioners who are technically trained in evaluation and who possess practical, political, and ethical savvy to guide us in conducting confirmative evaluation. Evaluators should also be keen listeners, solid diagnosticians, and effective problem solvers.
- Evaluation practitioners should view confirmative evaluation as a life-long learning initiative. It takes time to learn the technical skills; it takes a lifetime to practice those skills with diverse groups of people who possess special interests and unique needs.
- Evaluation practitioners need to form partnerships with organizations that are committed to the confirmative evaluation process. A synergistic relationship can be converted to benchmarking practices and give organizations a unique competitive edge.
- Evaluators, training, and HPT practitioners, sponsors, and stakeholders must be held accountable for what they do and do not do.

- When practitioners do a stellar job in overseeing a confirmative evaluation, budget monies can be justified. Although a budget for the evaluation is negotiated up front, it can be adjusted as time and deliverables prove a continuing need. The evaluator or training professional can conduct neither proactive nor reactive confirmative evaluation without a healthy budget.

- Practitioners need to become adept at doing more with less, especially in poor economic times when budget cuts and financial scrutiny are legion.

- Practitioners—and even stakeholders and sponsors—must begin to celebrate their successes in conducting a confirmative evaluation. A positive resolution can turn a negative outcome into a win-win situation for all.

- Practitioners should "use evaluation data only for continuous improvement and never for blaming" (Kaufman and Unger, 2003, p. 7).

Put Yourself in the Picture

Figure 9.1 presents some of the qualities that characterize a successful confirmative evaluator. The list is not all-inclusive; for example, the *planner* also has to be an organizer, the *doer* needs technical savvy, the *analyzer* requires perseverance, the *improver* should have the ability to facilitate relationships, and the *meta evaluator* must be a keen listener. PST 9.1 is a self-assessment to help you identify the personal qualities that make *you* a stellar confirmative evaluator.

Figure 9.1. Sample Qualities of a Stellar Confirmative Evaluator.

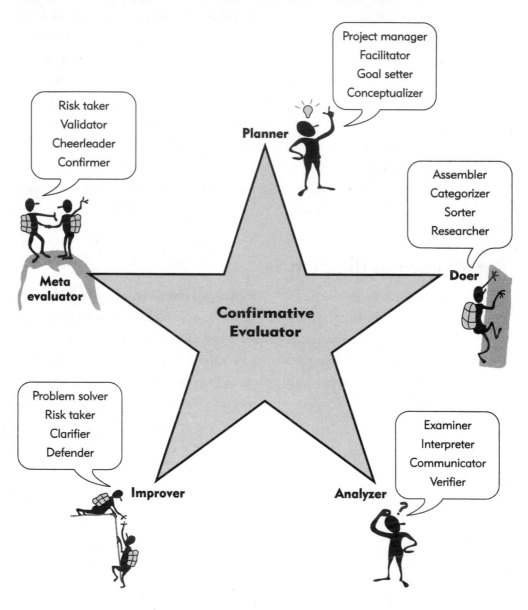

PST 9.1. Self-Assessment: Qualities of a Stellar Confirmative Evaluator.

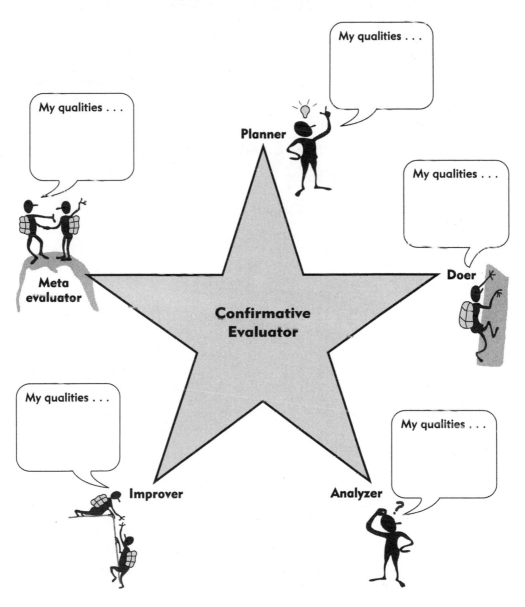

SUMMARY: LESSONS LEARNED IN CHAPTER NINE

1. There is an increased need for confirmative evaluation efforts.

2. The evaluation, training, or HPT practitioner is a change agent operating in the milieu of an emerging discipline.

3. Success in confirmative evaluation means knowing the territory and working with all audiences to make it relevant, realistic, and practical so that planned change can occur.

4. Confirmative evaluation is a lifelong learning process.

5. Personal lessons learned:

_____

_____

_____

_____

_____

_____

_____

_____

NEXT STEPS

This chapter ends the discussion on confirmative evaluation; however, we believe it is just the beginning of new challenges for evaluation, training, or HPT practitioners and the organizations they represent. Customer satisfaction, total quality, and continuous improvement will continue to make a difference for those who believe in confirmative evaluation and who risk doing it—and doing it well!

GLOSSARY

Although these terms are defined according to how they apply to training programs, they also apply to judging the merit, worth, or value of noninstructional performance-improvement interventions such as mentoring, reward and incentive programs, knowledge management systems, and others. Selected words within definitions are italicized to denote cross-reference to another entry.

Accountability Responsibility for results

ADDIE Traditional process model for instructional system design (*ISD*); stands for analyze, design, develop, implement, and evaluate

ADDI/E Variation of ADDIE process model for ISD, illustrating the integration of full-scope evaluation (E) throughout the ISD process

Alignment Degree to which training program goals and objectives and intended confirmative evaluation outputs and outcomes are in line with or synchronized with organizational mission, goals, and values

Analyze The confirmative evaluation event that involves studying the findings, discovering the meaning of the findings, and interpreting and reporting the results

Bottom line A reference to the emphasis on cost-effective rather than performance-effective training programs

Communication Sharing the progress and results of the confirmative evaluation with the stakeholders and the multiple audiences who need the information to improve performance

Communication technology Systematically applying knowledge gained from research into auditory, visual, and kinesthetic thinking, learning, and communication or message transmission

Confirmative evaluation Goes beyond formative and summative evaluation to judge the continued merit, value, or worth of a long-term training program

Confirmative evaluation plan Document that constitutes a blueprint for the evaluation, training, or HPT practitioner who conducts the confirmative evaluation and sells the evaluation to the stakeholders; includes an executive summary, an introduction, and a detailed plan for implementing the confirmative evaluation

Confirmative evaluation reports Documents that detail confirmative evaluation process, progress, and results; examples are announcements and releases, progress reports, interim or preliminary reports, final report

Consultant One role of the practitioner during confirmative evaluation; involves providing professional expertise as well as support for problem identification and problem solving

Context factors Past, current, or future situations within an organization that have a positive or negative effect on the successful initiation and completion of evaluation activities

Continuous improvement or continuous quality improvement (CQI) Ongoing, conscious efforts by an organization and its stakeholders to monitor, evaluate, maintain, or improve all performance-related activities; may include quality control of input and process and quality assurance of outputs and outcomes

Cost analysis Umbrella term for a set of analysis techniques that compare program costs with program benefits (cost-benefit analysis or CBA), effectiveness (cost-effectiveness analysis), usefulness (cost-utility analysis), or feasibility (cost-feasibility analysis)

Decision maker Person who charts the course of action or must approve implementation of a direction, process, product, commitment, and so forth, and may or may not supervise the process; one role of the evaluation, training, or HPT practitioner during confirmative evaluation

Descriptive design Describes or characterizes *evaluand* in basic terms (for example, frequency counts, time studies, cross-section designs)

Direct inputs Outputs or outcomes from a previous process or activity that are required by the system to initiate a process event; as an example, a statement of purpose is required to implement a successful confirmative evaluation

Do The confirmative evaluation event that involves collecting the data and documenting the findings

Education Instructional performance support system that develops knowledge, skills, and attitudes in individuals or groups; generally associated with K-12 and higher education

Effectiveness Degree to which a training program meets or exceeds the program goals and objectives and improves performance as much as possible

Efficiency Degree to which the productivity of a program exceeds its resource requirements; a program that is economical to deliver, uses as little off-the-job time as possible, and produces valuable results is considered efficient

Enabler One role of the practitioner during confirmative evaluation; helps and supports confirmative evaluation planning and implementation team

Enforcer One role of the practitioner during confirmative evaluation; actively monitors implementation of action plans

Evaluability assessment Identifying, recording, and rating the various evaluability factors or criteria that help determine whether it is possible and potentially valuable to conduct a confirmative evaluation of a specific training program

Evaluand Person, place, or thing that is being evaluated

Evaluation The process of judging the merit, value, or worth of a training program

Event An activity-based component of a process

Experimental design Formal approach to evaluation that validates the cause of the observed effect; includes random assignment of participants to training groups, and controls (equalizes) as many group factors as possible

Extant data analysis Technique of identifying and reviewing existing printed or electronic documents to retrieve information that is required to validate one or more intended evaluation outcomes

Feasibility Term used to describe whether a program or course of action is worth pursuing on the basis of an analysis of such factors as costs, benefits, resource capabilities, and risk

Formal evaluation Approach to evaluation that uses prescribed and systematic evaluation procedures and practices; for example, experimental or quasi-experimental evaluation designs

Formative evaluation Focuses on judging the merit, worth, or value of the processes used during the analysis, design, and development phases of instructional system design (*ISD*)

Full-scope evaluation A process that uses four types of evaluation (formative, summative, confirmative, and meta evaluation), if appropriate, to judge the merit, value, or worth of a training program or other performance improvement intervention

Gatekeeper for transfer Role of practitioner during training program planning and implementation; makes sure that the training program planners and implementers stay focused on both enablers and barriers to on-the-job transfer

Goodness Term used by the military and others to qualify the degree to which people, places, situations, or things meet stated or implicit standards for excellence and integrity

Impact Degree to which a training program has a positive or negative effect on individual, group, program, or organizational performance

Improve The confirmative evaluation event that focuses on making action decisions for continuous quality improvement on the basis of the results of the confirmative evaluation

Indirect inputs Inputs that are not the direct, tangible outputs of another process or process event; examples are commitment from stakeholders, or soft technologies, that support the success of the process, outputs, and outcomes of a system

Inferential statistics Statistical methods that validate whether a training program has the postulated or assumed effect on the individual, group, or organization

Informal evaluation Approach to evaluation that requires little preliminary planning; focuses on gathering anecdotal or self-reported information from people and documents; and results in few planned, long-range consequences (for example, naturalistic evaluation design)

Input Human and other resources required to initiate and complete a process

Instructional performance support systems Performance improvement support systems that are based on the transfer of knowledge, skills, and attitudes through education and training

Instructional system design or development (ISD) A process involving the systematic design and development of instruction (see *ADDIE* and *ADDI/E*)

Interpretation Discovering significance and implications from the analysis of data

Iterative model Illustration of a process that repeats itself as needed over time

Long-term effects In the case of confirmative evaluation, long-term effects of a training program are considered after the program is in operation for one or more years

Management by walking around (MBWA) A communication technique made famous by Tom Peters (with coauthors Robert H. Waterman, Jr., in *In Search of Excellence* and Nancy Austin in *A Passion for Excellence*); managers interact directly with workers to exchange information

Meta evaluation Judging the merit, worth, or value of an evaluation; type one meta evaluation is conducted concurrently with evaluation planning and implementation, and type two is conducted after formative, summative, and at least one cycle of confirmative evaluation are completed

Model Visual representation of a concept or process

Naturalistic evaluation design Informal approach to evaluation that assesses the value of a training program or other object by focusing on stakeholder perceptions, including but not limited to participant reactions, without manipulating or controlling the responses

Noninstructional performance support systems Performance improvement support systems that go beyond the transfer of knowledge, skills, and attitudes; examples are compensation plans, reward and incentive programs, mentoring, ergonomics, and others

Outcome The results or impact of a completed process

Output The products of a process; may or may not positively affect an outcome

Performance intervention Conscious, deliberate, planned change effort designed to improve human performance and solve workplace problems; the intervention may be a single effort (training) or a blended effort (for instance, combination of training, mentoring, and an incentive program)

Performance support tools Planned change efforts that sustain knowledge and skill transfer to the performer and from the performer to the job (for example, job aids, coaching programs, and so forth)

Plan The confirmative evaluation event that focuses on preparing a flexible blueprint for the confirmative evaluation: why, who, what, where, when, and how

Process What goes on (procedures) in a system between inputs and outputs to create the outputs and outcomes

Qualitative analysis Technique for examining and interpreting subjective data that are expressed primarily in written or spoken words; focuses on trends or patterns; presented as opinions, conclusions, ideas, and so forth

Quantitative analysis Techniques for examining and interpreting objective data that are expressed primarily in numbers (counts, ranks, percentages, and so forth)

Quasi-experimental design Formal approach to evaluation that is similar in form and function to experimental design but does not use random assignment to control for participant experience, entry-level knowledge, or other factors that affect the results of the intervention (training program)

Return on investment (ROI) analysis Analysis technique that places a tangible, monetary value on each program output and outcome (participant satisfaction, organizational benefits, and so forth) and compares the values with the cost of developing and implementing the program

Stakeholders Internal and external customers who have a vested interest (expressed as needs or expectations) in the process, outputs, and outcomes of a training program

Success syndrome Tendency of organizations or individuals to accept early positive reactions or results as a reason for *not* continuing with further evaluation plans

Summative evaluation Focuses on judging the merit, worth, or value of the immediate outputs of the implementation phase of *ISD*; may include evaluation of instructor and participant reactions; changes in participant knowledge, skills, or attitudes; and short-term transfer to the job

Technique Method used to perform an activity; examples are data-collection methods and data-analysis methods

Technology Systematically applying knowledge to improve performance; instructional technology (IT) and human performance technology (HPT) are commonly referred to as *soft* technologies; *hard* technology includes computers, telecommunications, and other man-machine interfaces

Tool Instrument such as a guide, script, form, questionnaire, and so forth, used to perform a technique

Total quality management (TQM) Umbrella term used to describe a process that views and manages quality from a variety of perspectives (quality assurance, continuous quality improvement, and so on)

Training Instructional performance support system that develops knowledge, skills, and attitudes in individuals or groups; provided to employees by employers

Transfer (on-the-job) Continuing application to the workplace reality of knowledge, skills, and attitudes learned during training

Utilization (utilitarian) evaluation Judging a training program on the basis of the merit, worth, and value of its utility (actual usefulness and impact); forms basis for decision making

Value Degree to which a training program increases the merit or worth of an individual, work group, or organization

Value-added A customer-focused perspective on quality ("Does this activity matter or have additional value for the customer?")

W^5H Organizational aid that prompts the user to identify and analyze who, what, where, when, why, and how before conducting an activity such as confirmative evaluation

REFERENCES

Alreck, P. L., and Settle, R. B. *The Survey Research Handbook: Guidelines and Strategies for Conducting a Survey.* Chicago: Irwin, 1995.

Banathy, B. H. *System Design of Education: A Journey to Create the Future.* Englewood Cliffs, N.J.: Educational Technology Publications, 1991.

Bassi, L., and Ahlstrand, A. *The 2000 ASTD Learning Outcomes Report: Second Annual Report on ASTD's Standards for Valuing Enterprises' Investments.* Alexandria, Va.: American Society for Training & Development, 2000.

Beer, V., and Bloomer, A. C. "Levels of Evaluation." *Educational Evaluation and Policy Analysis,* Winter 1986, *8*(4), 335–345.

Bergman, P., and Jacobson, H. "Yes, You Can Measure the Business Results of Training." *Training,* Aug. 2000, *37*(8), 68–72.

Bersin, J. "Measure the Metrics." *e-learning,* June 2002, *3*(6), 26–28.

Binder, C. "Measurement: A Few Important Ideas." *Performance Improvement,* 2001, *40*(3), 20–28.

Binder, C. "Commentary: An Open Letter to My Colleagues: How're We Doing?" *Performance Improvement,* 2002a, *41*(5), 6–9.

Binder, C. "Measurement Counts." *PerformanceXpress,* Mar. 2002b. (www.performancexpress.org/mainframe0203.html)

Binder, C. "Measurement Counts." *PerformanceXpress,* Apr. 2002c. (www.performancexpress.org/mainframe0204.html)

Boulmetis, J., and Dutwin, P. *The ABCs of Evaluation: Timeless Techniques for Program and Project Managers.* San Francisco: Jossey-Bass, 2000.

Brandenburg, D. C. "Evaluation and Business Issues: Tools for Management Decision Making." In R. O. Brinkerhoff (ed.), *Evaluating Training Programs in Business and Industry: New Directions for Program Evaluation.* San Francisco: Jossey-Bass, 1989.

Brinkerhoff, R. O. *Achieving Results from Training.* San Francisco: Jossey-Bass, 1987.

Brinkerhoff, R. O., and Apking, A. M. *High Impact Learning: Strategies for Leveraging Business Results from Training.* Cambridge: Mass.: Perseus, 2001.

Brinkerhoff, R. O., Brethower, D. M., Hluchyj, T., and Nowakowski, J. R. *Program Evaluation: A Practitioner's Guide for Trainers and Educators.* Boston: Kluwer-Nijhoff, 1983.

Carr, C. *Smart Training: The Manager's Guide to Training for Improved Performance.* New York: McGraw-Hill, 1992.

Coleman, S. D., Perry, J. D., and Schwen, T. M. "Constructivist Instructional Development: Reflecting on Practice from an Alternative Paradigm." In C. R. Dills and A. J. Romiszowski (eds.), *Instructional Development Paradigms.* Englewood Cliffs, N.J.: Educational Technology Publications, 1997.

Combs, W. L., and Falletta, S. V. *The Targeted Evaluation Process: A Performance Consultant's Guide to Asking the Right Questions and Getting the Results You Trust.* Alexandria, Va.: American Society for Training & Development, 2000.

Creelman, D. "What Does 'Value-Added' Mean?" *PerformanceXpress,* Feb. 2002. (www.performance.org)

Daft, R. L. *Management* (4th ed.). Fort Worth: Dryden Press, 1997.

Dessinger, J. C. "What You Said Would Happen Has Happened (aka Confirmative Evaluation)." (Crackerbarrel presentation handout). Fortieth Annual International Performance Improvement Conference and Expo, Dallas, Apr. 23, 2002.

Dick, W. "Quality in Training Organizations." *Performance Improvement Quarterly,* 1993, *6*(3), 35–47.

Dick, W., and King, D. "Formative Evaluation in the Performance Context." *Performance and Instruction,* 1994, *33*(9), 8.

Dixon, N. M. *Evaluation: A Tool for Improving HRD Quality.* San Francisco: Pfeiffer; Alexandria, Va.: American Society for Training & Development, 1990.

Esque, T. J. *Making an Impact: Building a Top-Performing Organization from the Bottom Up.* Atlanta: CEP Press; Silver Spring, Md.: International Society for Performance Improvement, 2001.

Fink, A. *Evaluation Fundamentals: Guiding Health Programs, Research, and Policy.* Thousand Oaks, Calif.: Sage, 1993.

Fink, A. *How to Analyze Survey Data.* Thousand Oaks, Calif.: Sage, 1995.

Fitz-Gibbon, C. T., and Morris, L. L. *How to Design a Program Evaluation.* Thousand Oaks, Calif.: Sage, 1987.

Fitzpatrick, J. L., Sanders, J. R., & Worthen, B. R. *Program Evaluation: Alternative Approaches and Practical Guidelines* (3rd ed.). Boston: Pearson/Allyn and Bacon, 2004.

Geis, G. L., and Smith, M. E. "The Function of Evaluation." In H. D. Stolovitch and E. J. Keeps (eds.), *Handbook of Human Performance Technology.* Silver Spring, Md.: International Society for Performance and Improvement, 1992.

Ghattas, R. G., and McKee, S. L. *Practical Project Management.* Upper Saddle River, N.J.: Prentice Hall, 2001.

Gibson, J. L., Ivancevich, J. M., and Donnelly, J. J., Jr. *Organizations: Behavior, Structure, Processes* (9th ed.). Chicago: Irwin, 1997.

Gilbert, T. F. *Human Competence: Engineering Worthy Performance.* Washington, D.C.: International Society for Performance Improvement, 1996.

Greenagel, F. L. "The Illusion of E-learning: Why We Are Missing Out on the Promise of IP Technology." July 31, 2002. (www.elearningmag.com/elearning/article/articleDetail.jsp?id=26850)

Greer, M. *ID Project Management: Tools and Techniques for Instructional Designers and Developers.* Englewood Cliffs, N.J.: Educational Technology Publications, 1992.

Hale, J. *Performance-Based Evaluation: Tools and Techniques to Measure the Impact of Training.* San Francisco: Jossey-Bass/Pfeiffer, 2002a.

Hale, J. "Performance-Based Evaluation: Why Another Book?" *PerformanceXpress,* Aug. 2002b. (www.performancexpress.org/sep02.html)

Hannum, W., and Hansen, C. *Instructional Systems Development in Large Organizations.* Englewood Cliffs, N.J.: Educational Technology Publications, 1989.

Hanson, R. A., and Siegel, D. F. "The Three Phases of Evaluation: Formative, Summative, and Confirmative." Updated draft of paper originally presented at the 1991 meeting of the American Educational Research Association, Chicago, Apr. 3–7, 1995.

Hatry, H. P., Newcomer, K. E., and Wholey, J. S. "Conclusion: Improving Evaluation Activities and Results." In J. S. Wholey, H. P. Hatry, and K. E. Newcomer (eds.), *Handbook of Practical Program Evaluation.* San Francisco: Jossey-Bass, 1994.

Heinich, R., Molenda, M., Russell, J. D., and Smaldino, S. E. *Instructional Media and Technologies for Learning* (5th ed.). Upper Saddle River, N.J.: Prentice Hall, 1996.

Hellebrandt, J., and Russell, J. D. "Confirmative Evaluation of Instructional Materials and Learners." *Performance and Instruction,* July 1993, *32*(6), 22–27.

Hodges, T. K. *Linking Learning and Performance: A Practical Guide to Measuring Learning and On-the-Job Application.* Boston: Butterworth Heinemann, 2002.

Jackson, T. *Evaluation: Relating Training to Business Performance.* San Francisco: Pfeiffer, 1989.

The Joint Committee on Standards for Educational Evaluation. *The Program Evaluation Standards: How to Assess Evaluation of Educational Programs* (2nd ed.). Thousand Oaks, Calif.: Sage, 1994.

Kaufman, R., Keller, J., and Watkins, R. "What Works and What Doesn't: Evaluation Beyond Kirkpatrick." *Performance and Instruction,* 1996, *35*(2), 8–12.

Kaufman, R., Rojas, A. M., and Mayer, H. *Needs Assessment: A User's Guide.* Englewood Cliffs, N.J.: Educational Technology Publications, 1993.

Kaufman, R., & Unger, Z. "Evaluation Plus: Beyond Conventional Evaluation." *Performance Improvement,* 2003, *42*(7), 5–8.

Kee, J. E. "Benefit-Cost Analysis in Program Evaluation." In J. S. Wholey, H. P. Hatry, and K. E. Newcomer (eds.), *Handbook of Practical Program Evaluation.* San Francisco: Jossey-Bass, 1994.

Kemp, J. E., and Cochern, G. W. *Planning for Effective Technical Training: A Guide for Instructors and Trainers.* Englewood Cliffs, N.J.: Educational Technology Publications, 1994.

Kirkpatrick, D. L. "Techniques for Evaluating Training Programs." *Journal of the American Society of Training Directors,* Nov.–Dec. 1959, *13,* 3ff.

Kirkpatrick, D. L. "Techniques for Evaluating Training Programs." *Journal of the American Society of Training Directors,* Jan.–Feb. 1960, *14,* 13ff.

Kirkpatrick, D. L. *Evaluating Training Programs: The Four Levels.* San Francisco: Berrett-Koehler, 1994.

Korth, S. J. "Consolidating Needs Assessment and Evaluation." *Performance Improvement,* 2001, *40*(1), 38–43.

Levin, H. M. *Cost-Effectiveness: A Primer.* Thousand Oaks, Calif.: Sage, 1983.

Lindsley, O. "From Training Evaluation to Performance Tracking." In H. D. Stolovitch and E. J. Keeps (eds.), *Handbook of Human Performance Technology: Improving Individual and Organizational Performance Worldwide* (2nd ed.). San Francisco: Jossey-Bass/Pfeiffer, 1999.

Lipps, G., and Grant, P. R. "A Participatory Method of Assessing Program Implementation." *Evaluation Review,* Aug. 1990, *14*(4), 427–434.

Mark, M. M., and Pines, E. "Implications of Continuous Quality Improvement for Program Evaluation and Evaluators." *Evaluation Practice,* 1995, *16*(2), 131–139.

McKenzie, J. F., and Smeltzer, J. L. *Planning, Implementing and Evaluating Health Promotion Programs. A Primer* (3rd ed.). Boston: Allyn and Bacon, 2001.

Misanchuk, E. R. "Descriptors of Evaluation in Instructional Development: Beyond the Formative-Summative Distinction." *Journal of Instructional Development,* 1978, *2*(1), 15–19.

Morris, L. L., and Fitz-Gibbon, C. T. *How to Present an Evaluation Report.* Thousand Oaks, Calif.: Sage, 1978.

Moseley, J. L. "So You Want to Evaluate a Program? Seven Steps to Make It Happen." (Crackerbarrel presentation handout). Fortieth Annual International Performance Improvement Conference and Expo, Dallas, Apr. 23, 2002.

Moseley, J. L., and Dessinger, J. C. "The Dessinger-Moseley 360° Evaluation Model: A Comprehensive Approach to Training Evaluation." In P. J. Dean and D. E. Ripley (eds.), *Performance Improvement Interventions: Instructional Design and Training (Vol. 2).* Washington, D.C.: International Society for Performance Improvement, 1998.

Moseley, J. L., and Solomon, D. L. "Confirmative Evaluation: A New Paradigm for Continuous Improvement." *Performance Improvement,* 1997, *36*(5), 12–16.

Oermann, M. H., and Gaberson, K. B. *Evaluation and Testing in Nursing Education.* New York: Springer, 1998.

Parkman, A. W. "Performance Consulting: The Beginning of the ROI Process." *PerformanceXpress,* Feb. 2002. (www.performancexpress.org/0202/)

Patterson, K., Grenny, J., McMillan, R., and Swizler, A. *Better Than Duct Tape: Dialogue Tools for Getting Results.* Plano, Tex.: Pritchett Rummler-Brache, 2000.

Patton, M. Q. *How to Use Qualitative Methods in Evaluation.* Thousand Oaks, Calif.: Sage, 1987.

Patton, M. Q. *Utilization Focused Evaluation: The New Century Text* (3rd ed.). Thousand Oaks, Calif.: Sage, 1997.

Phillips, J. J. *Handbook of Training Evaluation and Measurement Methods* (3rd ed.). Houston: Gulf, 1997a.

Phillips, J. J. *Return on Investment in Training and Performance Improvement Programs* (2nd ed.). St. Louis, Mo: Elsevier, 2003.

Phillips, J. J., and Hodges, T. *Measuring the Return on Investment in Human Resource Development.* (Presentation handout). American Society for Training & Development International Conference and Expo, Atlanta, May 24, 1999.

Phillips, J., Pulliam, P. F., and Wurtz, W. *Level 5 Evaluation: ROI* (*Info-line,* no. 9805). Alexandria, Va.: American Society for Training & Development, May 1998.

Posavac, E. J., and Carey, R. G. *Program Evaluation: Methods and Case Studies* (3rd ed.). Upper Saddle River, N.J.: Prentice Hall, 1989.

Rae, L. *Using Evaluation in Training and Development.* London: Kogan Page, 1999.

Reed, S. O. "The New Organization and Implications for Training." *Performance Improvement,* May–June 2002, *41*(5), 24–28.

Robinson, D. G. "Training for Impact: How to Stop Spinning Your Wheels and Get into the Race." *Training,* Feb. 1984, *21*(2), 42–47.

Robinson, D. G., and Robinson, J. C. *Training for Impact: How to Link Training to Business Needs and Measure the Results.* San Francisco: Jossey-Bass, 1989.

Rossett, A. *Training Needs Assessment.* Englewood Cliffs, N.J.: Educational Technology Publications, 1987.

Rossett, A. *First Things Fast.* San Francisco: Jossey-Bass/Pfeiffer, 1999.

Rossi, P. H., and Freeman, H. E. *Evaluation: A Systematic Approach* (5th ed.). Thousand Oaks, Calif.: Sage, 1993.

Rossi, P. H., Freeman, H. E., and Lipsey, M. W. *Evaluation: A Systematic Approach* (6th ed.). Thousand Oaks, Calif.: Sage, 1999.

Rossman, G. B., and Rallis, S. F. "Critical Inquiry and Use as Action." In V. J. Caracelli and H. Preskill (eds.), *The Expanding Scope of Evaluation Use.* San Francisco: Jossey-Bass, with American Evaluation Association, 2000.

Rothwell, W. J. *Beyond Training and Development: State of the Art Strategies for Enhancing Human Performance.* New York: AMACOM, 1996.

Russ-Eft, D., and Preskill, H. *Evaluation in Organizations: A Systematic Approach to Enhancing Learning, Performance, and Change.* Cambridge, Mass.: Perseus, 2001.

Sanders, E. "Where Learning Technologies and ISD Meet." *Technical Training,* May-June 1999, *10*(3), 36.

Schalock, R. *Outcome-Based Evaluation.* New York: Plenum Press, 1995.

Schmidt, L. "In Practice: Using a Training Scorecard to Prove Training Pays." *ASTD LINKS,* Sept. 2002. (www1.astd.org/news_letter/September/Links/in_practice_scorecard.html)

Scriven, M. "The Methodology of Evaluation." In R. Tyler, R. Gagne, and M. Scriven (eds.), *AERA Monograph Series on Curriculum Evaluation: Perspectives of Curriculum Evaluation.* Chicago: Rand McNally, 1967.

Seels, B. B., and Richey, R. C. *Instructional Technology: The Definition and Domains of the Field.* Bloomington, Ind.: Association for Educational Communication and Technology, 1994.

Senge, P. *The Fifth Discipline: The Art and Practice of the Learning Organization.* New York: Doubleday, 1990.

Shank, P. "What Newbies Don't Know." *OnLine Learning News,* Oct. 1, 2001, *4*(29). (www.OLNews@vnulearning.com)

Shrock, S. A., and Geis, G. L. "Evaluation." In H. D. Stolovitch and E. J. Keeps (eds.), *Handbook of Human Performance Technology: Improving Individual and Organizational Performance Worldwide* (2nd ed.). San Francisco: Jossey-Bass/Pfeiffer; Silver Spring, Md: International Society for Performance and Instruction, 1999.

Smith, M. E., and Brandenburg, D. C. "Summative Evaluation." *Performance Improvement Quarterly,* 1991, *4*(2), 35–58.

Smith, M. F. *Evaluability Assessment: A Practical Approach.* Boston: Kluwer, 1989.

Sonnichsen, R. C. "Evaluators as Change Agents." In J. S. Wholey, H. P. Hatry, and K. E. Newcomer (eds.), *Handbook of Practical Program Evaluation.* San Francisco: Jossey-Bass, 1994.

Spitzer, D. "IBM Learning Effectiveness Measurement (LEM)." Presentation at the Fortieth Annual International Society for Performance Improvement Conference and Expo, Dallas, Apr. 23, 2002.

Spitzer, D., and Conway, M. "Link Training to Your Bottom Line." (*Info-line,* no. 0201.) Alexandria, Va.: American Society for Training & Development, Jan. 2002.

Stufflebeam, D. "Meta Evaluation: An Overview." *Evaluation and the Health Professions,* 1978, *1*, 17–43.

Swanson, R. A. *Analysis for Improving Performance.* San Francisco: Berrett-Koehler, 1994.

Swanson, R. A. "Background Research in Human Resource Development." In R. L. Craig (ed.), *The ASTD Training & Development Handbook* (4th ed.). New York: McGraw Hill, 1996.

Tessmer, M. "Formative Evaluation Alternatives." *Performance Improvement Quarterly,* 1994, *7*(1), 3–18.

Thiagarajan, S. "Formative Evaluation in Performance Technology." *Performance Improvement Quarterly,* 1991, *4*(2), 22–34.

Tracey, M. W., Solomon, D. L., and Moseley, J. L. "Professional Development and Dialogue: A 90-Minute Experiential Approach." Unpublished manuscript.

Van Tiem, D. M., Moseley, J. L., and Dessinger, J. C. *Fundamentals of Performance Technology: A Guide to Improving People, Process, and Performance.* Washington, D.C.: International Society for Performance Improvement, 2000.

Van Tiem, D. M., Moseley, J. L., and Dessinger, J. C. *Performance Improvement Interventions: Enhancing People, Processes, and Organizations Through*

Performance Technology. Silver Spring, Md.: International Society for Performance Improvement, 2001.

Wang, G. "Control Group Methods for HPT Program Evaluation and Measurement." *Performance Improvement Quarterly,* 2002, *15*(2), 34–48.

Watkins, R., and Kaufman, R. "Assessing and Evaluating: Differentiating Perspectives." *Performance Improvement,* 2002, *41*(2), 22–28.

Wholey, J. S. "Assessing the Feasibility and Likely Usefulness of Evaluation." In J. S. Wholey, H. P. Hatry, and K. E. Newcomer (eds.), *Handbook of Practical Program Evaluation.* San Francisco: Jossey-Bass, 1994.

Wholey, J. S., Hatry, H. P., and Newcomer, K. E. (eds.). *Handbook of Practical Program Evaluation.* San Francisco: Jossey-Bass, 1994.

Wilson, B. "Get into My House." *ASTD What Works! E-Newsletter,* May 23, 2002. (ASTD@knowledge-media.com)

Windsor, R., Baranowski, T., Clark, N., and Cutter, G. *Evaluation of Health Promotion, Health Education and Disease Prevention Programs* (2nd ed.). Mountain View, Calif.: Mayfield, 1994.

Worthen, B. R., and Sanders, J. R. *Educational Evaluation: Alternative Approaches and Practical Guidelines.* White Plains, N.Y.: Longman, 1987.

Worthen, B. R., Sanders, J. R., and Fitzpatrick, J. L. *Program Evaluation: Alternative Approaches and Practical Guidelines* (2nd ed.). White Plains, N.Y.: Longman, 1997.

Zemke, R., and Kramlinger, T. *Figuring Things Out: A Trainer's Guide to Needs and Task Analysis.* Reading, Mass.: Addison-Wesley, 1987.

INDEX

Joan Conway Dessinger is principal with the Lake Group, a performance consulting firm. She earned an Ed.D. in Instructional Technology from Wayne State University and is a certified performance technologist (CPT). Her clients have included Chrysler, Dow Chemical, Enrico Fermi Nuclear Plant, Ford Motor, General Motors, NEC Technologies, Pioneer Hybrid International, Procter and Gamble, Raytheon, Saturn, and Sterling Drugs. She has also taught graduate courses in adult learning; instructional system analysis, design, evaluation, and project management; curriculum planning; and administration of health education/promotion programs at Wayne State University, Central Michigan University, University of Detroit-Mercy College of Health Sciences, and Madonna University.

Dessinger has coauthored two books: *Fundamentals of Performance Technology: A Guide to Improving People, Process, and Performance* and *Performance Improvement Interventions: Enhancing People, Process, and Organizations Through Performance Technology.* Both won ISPI Awards of Excellence for Communication. She also coauthored a chapter on evaluation for the *Performance*

Improvement Series Volume Two: Performance Improvement Interventions; a chapter on evaluating satellite-based distance training for *Distance Training* (1998, Jossey-Bass); and a chapter on the FORDSTAR distance learning program at Ford for *Sustaining Distance Training* (2001, Jossey-Bass). She has published journal articles on analysis, evaluation, job performance aids, the late-life learner, satellite distance training, and performance technology.

Dessinger is a member of the International Society for Performance Improvement (ISPI) and the American Society for Training & Development (ASTD) and has presented at local, national, and international conferences.

James L. Moseley is associate professor of community medicine at Wayne State University School of Medicine, where he teaches health administration courses. He also enjoys full associate graduate faculty status in the College of Education, where he teaches and directs dissertations on performance improvement. In a previous life, he was a successful high school teacher, a director of guidance and counseling, and a principal of two high schools.

Moseley has an extensive publication record of journal articles, book chapters, and proceedings. He coauthored *Fundamentals of Performance Technology: A Guide to Improving People, Process, and Performance* and *Performance Improvement Interventions: Enhancing People, Process, and Organizations Through Performance Technology*. Both books have won the Outstanding Instructional Communication Award of Excellence from the ISPI. He has conducted numerous workshops at professional national and international meetings.

Moseley attended classes at the University of Detroit, the Merrill-Palmer Institute of Family Life and Human Development, Sacred Heart Seminary, Wayne State University, Central Michigan University, and Harvard University. He holds Ed.D, Ed.S, M.A., M.S.L.S., M.Ed., and M.S.A. degrees. He is a licensed professional counselor (LPC), a certified health education specialist (CHES), and a certified performance technologist (CPT); he also holds other licenses and certificates. He is a past president of both the Michigan Society of Gerontology and the International Society of WORKSHOP WAY Educators.

 **Rita C. Richey** is professor and program coordinator of instructional technology at Wayne State University. She has been at Wayne State for over thirty years and is experienced in not only program development, but also in education and training research. She has published widely in the areas of instructional design theory, including such books as *The Theoretical and Conceptual Bases of Instructional Design, Designing Instruction for the Adult Learner,* and *The Legacy of Robert M. Gagne.* Rita is coauthor of the third edition of *Instructional Design Competencies: The Standards* and the third edition of *Training Manager Competencies: The Standards.* She is also coauthor of *Instructional Technology: The Definition and Domains of the Field,* a book that received the 1995 Outstanding Book Award and the 1996 Brown Publication Award, both from the Association of Educational Communications and Technology. She has also received four major awards from Wayne State University: the President's Award for Excellence in Teaching, the Outstanding Graduate Mentor's Award, a Distinguished Faculty Fellowship, and an

award for Outstanding Scholarly Achievement by Women Faculty. In addition, she has been elected to the Wayne State University Academy of Scholars. In recognition of her career's work, she received the AECT Distinguished Service Award in 2000.

 **William J. Rothwell**, Ph.D., SPHR certification, is professor in charge of the workforce education and development program in the Department of Learning and Performance Systems at Pennsylvania State University. He is also president of Rothwell and Associates, Inc., an independent consulting firm. He has been a training director in a government agency and a large insurance company, a consultant to many organizations, and a college professor.

William is the author and coauthor of many books. His most recent publications include *Mastering the Instructional Design Process: A Systematic Approach,* 3rd edition (with H.C. Kazanas, 2004), *The Strategic Development of Talent* (with H.C. Kazanas, 2003), *What CEOs Expect from Corporate Training: Building Workplace Learning and Performance Initiatives That Advance Organizational Goals* (with J. Lindholm and W. Wallick, 2003), *Planning and Managing Human Resources,* 2nd edition (with H.C. Kazanas, 2003), *Creating Sales Training and Development Programs: A Competency-Based Approach to Building Sales Ability* (with W. Donahue and J. Park, 2002), *The Workplace Learner: How to Align Training Initiatives with Individual Learning Competencies* (2002), and *Building Effective Technical Training: How to Develop Hard Skills Within Organizations* (with J. Benkowski, 2002).

In his consulting work, William specializes in human resources practices—particularly in competency modeling and succession planning and management.

Timothy W. Spannaus, Ph.D., is senior lecturer in instructional technology and research fellow with the Institute for Learning and Performance Improvement, at Wayne State University. He is also chief learning architect at The Emdicium Group, Inc., in Southfield, Michigan.

Tim is president of the International Board of Standards for Training, Performance, and Instruction and was previously president of the Association for Development of Computer-Based Instructional Systems. He is active in the International Society for Performance Improvement and the American Society for Training and Development.

His teaching, research, and development focus on interactive technologies for learning and performance improvement. Recent projects include the creation of a training vision for a major municipal utility, the design and development of web-based learning courses, and a knowledge management plan for a Fortune 500 manufacturer. Recent publications include *Training Manager Competencies: The Standards,* two chapters in the *ID Casebook*—a forthcoming book on development of web-based learning—and numerous papers and presentations.

Kent L. Gustafson, Ph.D., is professor emeritus of instructional technology at the University of Georgia, where he was chair of the department and taught courses in instructional design, research, and management of technology-based education programs. He has published three books and numerous articles, book chapters, and technical reports. Kent is a regular presenter at major educational conferences in the United States and has spoken in many other countries including Australia, Iran, Japan, Korea, the Netherlands, Malaysia, Mexico, Nicaragua, the Philippines, and Switzerland. He is also former president of the Association for Educational Communications and Technology. Kent's research interest includes design and evaluation of electronic performance support systems, management of technology design and delivery, and professional education of technologists.

M. David Merrill, Ph.D., is professor in the department of instructional technology at Utah State University. He is also the owner and president of Ascape, Tennsion & Sulphur Gulch RR. Recognized as a leader in instructional design,

David is listed among the most productive educational psychologists (*Educational Researcher,* 1984), the most frequently cited authors in the computer-based instruction literature (*Journal of Computer-Based Instruction,* 1987), and the most influential people in the field of instructional technology (*Performance & Instruction,* 1988.) As a major contributor in his field, David was the recipient of the Association for Educational Communications and Technology's 2001 Distinguished Service Award for advancing the field of instructional technology through scholarship, teaching, and leadership. His current work involves the identification of First Principles of Instruction.

Allison Rossett, Ed.D., is professor of educational technology at San Diego State University, with academic focus on workforce development, e-learning, and needs assessment. Allison received the American Society for Training and Development's award for Workplace Learning and Performance for 2002 and will join its International Board in January 2004. She is also a member of *Training* magazine's HRD Hall of Fame, the editor of the *ASTD E-Learning Handbook: Best Practices, Strategies, and Case Studies for an Emerging Field,* and co-author of *Beyond the Podium: Delivering Training and Performance to a Digital World.* Allison has worked with a who's who of international organizations, including IBM, Microsoft, MetLife, the Internal Revenue Service, Hewlett-Packard, SQL Star International, Ford Motor Company, SBC, and Fidelity Investments.

Pfeiffer Publications Guide

This guide is designed to familiarize you with the various types of Pfeiffer publications. The formats section describes the various types of products that we publish; the methodologies section describes the many different ways that content might be provided within a product. We also provide a list of the topic areas in which we publish.

FORMATS

In addition to its extensive book-publishing program, Pfeiffer offers content in an array of formats, from fieldbooks for the practitioner to complete, ready-to-use training packages that support group learning.

FIELDBOOK Designed to provide information and guidance to practitioners in the midst of action. Most fieldbooks are companions to another, sometimes earlier, work, from which its ideas are derived; the fieldbook makes practical what was theoretical in the original text. Fieldbooks can certainly be read from cover to cover. More likely, though, you'll find yourself bouncing around following a particular theme, or dipping in as the mood, and the situation, dictate.

HANDBOOK A contributed volume of work on a single topic, comprising an eclectic mix of ideas, case studies, and best practices sourced by practitioners and experts in the field.

An editor or team of editors usually is appointed to seek out contributors and to evaluate content for relevance to the topic. Think of a handbook not as a ready-to-eat meal, but as a cookbook of ingredients that enables you to create the most fitting experience for the occasion.

RESOURCE Materials designed to support group learning. They come in many forms: a complete, ready-to-use exercise (such as a game); a comprehensive resource on one topic (such as conflict management) containing a variety of methods and approaches; or a collection of like-minded activities (such as icebreakers) on multiple subjects and situations.

TRAINING PACKAGE An entire, ready-to-use learning program that focuses on a particular topic or skill. All packages comprise a guide for the facilitator/trainer and a workbook for the participants. Some packages are supported with additional media—such as video—or learning aids, instruments, or other devices to help participants understand concepts or practice and develop skills.

- *Facilitator/trainer's guide* Contains an introduction to the program, advice on how to organize and facilitate the learning event, and step-by-step instructor notes. The guide also contains copies of presentation materials—handouts, presentations, and overhead designs, for example—used in the program.

• *Participant's workbook* Contains exercises and reading materials that support the learning goal and serves as a valuable reference and support guide for participants in the weeks and months that follow the learning event. Typically, each participant will require his or her own workbook.

ELECTRONIC CD-ROMs and web-based products transform static Pfeiffer content into dynamic, interactive experiences. Designed to take advantage of the searchability, automation, and ease-of-use that technology provides, our e-products bring convenience and immediate accessibility to your workspace.

METHODOLOGIES

CASE STUDY A presentation, in narrative form, of an actual event that has occurred inside an organization. Case studies are not prescriptive, nor are they used to prove a point; they are designed to develop critical analysis and decision-making skills. A case study has a specific time frame, specifies a sequence of events, is narrative in structure, and contains a plot structure—an issue (what should be/have been done?). Use case studies when the goal is to enable participants to apply previously learned theories to the circumstances in the case, decide what is pertinent, identify the real issues, decide what should have been done, and develop a plan of action.

ENERGIZER A short activity that develops readiness for the next session or learning event. Energizers are most commonly used after a break or lunch to stimulate or refocus the group. Many involve some form of physical activity, so they are a useful way to counter post-lunch lethargy. Other uses include transitioning from one topic to another, where "mental" distancing is important.

EXPERIENTIAL LEARNING ACTIVITY (ELA) A facilitator-led intervention that moves participants through the learning cycle from experience to application (also known as a Structured Experience). ELAs are carefully thought-out designs in which there is a definite learning purpose and intended outcome. Each step—everything that participants do during the activity—facilitates the accomplishment of the stated goal. Each ELA includes complete instructions for facilitating the intervention and a clear statement of goals, suggested group size and timing, materials required, an explanation of the process, and, where appropriate, possible variations to the activity. (For more detail on Experiential Learning Activities, see the Introduction to the *Reference Guide to Handbooks and Annuals*, 1999 edition, Pfeiffer, San Francisco.)

GAME A group activity that has the purpose of fostering team spirit and togetherness in addition to the achievement of a pre-stated goal. Usually contrived—undertaking a desert expedition, for example—this type of learning method offers an engaging means for participants to demonstrate and practice business and interpersonal skills. Games are effective for team building and personal development mainly because the goal is subordinate to the process—the means through which participants reach decisions, collaborate, communicate, and generate trust and understanding. Games often engage teams in "friendly" competition.

ICEBREAKER A (usually) short activity designed to help participants overcome initial anxiety in a training session and/or to acquaint the participants with one another. An icebreaker can be a fun activity or can be tied to specific topics or training goals. While a useful tool in itself, the icebreaker comes into its own in situations where tension or resistance exists within a group.

INSTRUMENT A device used to assess, appraise, evaluate, describe, classify, and summarize various aspects of human behavior. The term used to describe an instrument depends primarily on its format and purpose. These terms include survey, questionnaire, inventory, diagnostic, survey, and poll. Some uses of instruments include providing instrumental feedback to group members, studying here-and-now processes or functioning within a group, manipulating group composition, and evaluating outcomes of training and other interventions.

Instruments are popular in the training and HR field because, in general, more growth can occur if an individual is provided with a method for focusing specifically on his or her own behavior. Instruments also are used to obtain information that will serve as a basis for change and to assist in workforce planning efforts.

Paper-and-pencil tests still dominate the instrument landscape with a typical package comprising a facilitator's guide, which offers advice on administering the instrument and interpreting the collected data, and an initial set of instruments. Additional instruments are available separately. Pfeiffer, though, is investing heavily in e-instruments. Electronic instrumentation provides effortless distribution and, for larger groups particularly, offers advantages over paper-and-pencil tests in the time it takes to analyze data and provide feedback.

LECTURETTE A short talk that provides an explanation of a principle, model, or process that is pertinent to the participants' current learning needs. A lecturette is intended to establish a common language bond between the trainer and the participants by providing a mutual frame of reference. Use a lecturette as an introduction to a group activity or event, as an interjection during an event, or as a handout.

MODEL A graphic depiction of a system or process and the relationship among its elements. Models provide a frame of reference and something more tangible, and more easily remembered, than a verbal explanation. They also give participants something to "go on," enabling them to track their own progress as they experience the dynamics, processes, and relationships being depicted in the model.

ROLE PLAY A technique in which people assume a role in a situation/scenario: a customer service rep in an angry-customer exchange, for example. The way in which the role is approached is then discussed and feedback is offered. The role play is often repeated using a different approach and/or incorporating changes made based on feedback received. In other words, role playing is a spontaneous interaction involving realistic behavior under artificial (and safe) conditions.

SIMULATION A methodology for understanding the interrelationships among components of a system or process. Simulations differ from games in that they test or use a model that depicts or mirrors some aspect of reality in form, if not necessarily in content. Learning occurs by studying the effects of change on one or more factors of the model. Simulations are commonly used to test hypotheses about what happens in a system—often referred to as "what if?" analysis—or to examine best-case/worst-case scenarios.

THEORY A presentation of an idea from a conjectural perspective. Theories are useful because they encourage us to examine behavior and phenomena through a different lens.

TOPICS

The twin goals of providing effective and practical solutions for workforce training and organization development and meeting the educational needs of training and human resource professionals shape Pfeiffer's publishing program. Core topics include the following:

> Leadership & Management
>
> Communication & Presentation
>
> Coaching & Mentoring
>
> Training & Development
>
> E-Learning
>
> Teams & Collaboration
>
> OD & Strategic Planning
>
> Human Resources
>
> Consulting

What will you find on pfeiffer.com?

• The best in workplace performance solutions for training and HR professionals

• Downloadable training tools, exercises, and content

• Web-exclusive offers

• Training tips, articles, and news

• Seamless on-line ordering

• Author guidelines, information on becoming a Pfeiffer Affiliate, and much more

Discover more at www.pfeiffer.com

Customer Care

Have a question, comment, or suggestion? Contact us! We value your feedback and we want to hear from you.

For questions about this or other Pfeiffer products, you may contact us by:

E-mail: **customer@wiley.com**

Mail: **Customer Care Wiley/Pfeiffer**
10475 Crosspoint Blvd.
Indianapolis, IN 46256

Phone: **(US) 800-274-4434** (Outside the US: 317-572-3985)

Fax: **(US) 800-569-0443** (Outside the US: 317-572-4002)

To order additional copies of this title or to browse other Pfeiffer products, visit us online at **www.pfeiffer.com**.

For **Technical Support** questions, call **(800) 274-4434.**

For authors guidelines, log on to www.pfeiffer.com and click on "Resources for Authors."

If you are . . .

A **college bookstore, a professor, an instructor, or work in higher education** and you'd like to place an order or request an exam copy, please contact jbreview@wiley.com.

A **general retail bookseller** and you'd like to establish an account or speak to a local sales representative, contact Melissa Grecco at 201-748-6267 or mgrecco@wiley.com.

An **exclusively on-line bookseller**, contact Amy Blanchard at 530-756-9456 or ablanchard@wiley.com or Jennifer Johnson at 206-568-3883 or jjohnson@wiley.com, both of our Online Sales department.

A **librarian or library representative**, contact John Chambers in our Library Sales department at 201-748-6291 or jchamber@wiley.com.

A **reseller, training company/consultant, or corporate trainer**, contact Charles Regan in our Special Sales department at 201-748-6553 or cregan@wiley.com.

A **specialty retail distributor** (includes specialty gift stores, museum shops, and corporate bulk sales), contact Kim Hendrickson in our Special Sales department at 201-748-6037 or khendric@wiley.com.

Purchasing for the **Federal government**, contact Ron Cunningham in our Special Sales department at 317-572-3053 or rcunning@wiley.com.

Purchasing for a **State or Local government**, contact Charles Regan in our Special Sales department at 201-748-6553 or cregan@wiley.com.

Cornerstones of Freedom

The Story of
THE BATTLE
OF THE BULGE

By R. Conrad Stein

Illustrated by Lou Aronson

CHILDRENS PRESS, CHICAGO

Library of Congress Cataloging in Publication Data

Stein, R   Conrad.
   The story of the Battle of the Bulge.

   (Cornerstones of freedom)
   SUMMARY: Details the Germans' last big offensive
to reverse the course of World War II at the end
of 1944.
   1. Ardennes, Battle of the 1944-1945—Juvenile
literature. [1. Ardennes, Battle of the, 1944-1945.
2. World War, 1939-1945—Campaigns] I. Aronson,
Lou. II. Title
D756.5.A7S74   940.54'21   77-5431
ISBN 0-516-04608-X

There are times in battle when both sides are resting and the mood is quiet. Early December, 1944, in the Ardennes Forest was one of those times. Snow decorated the trees in this lovely pine forest where the borders of Germany, Belgium, and Luxembourg all come together. On each side of a loosely determined battle line, groups of German and American soldiers were building fires and eating from mess kits. They could see each other and could have fired, but chose not to disturb this moment of peace in what had been a long, long war.

Besides, the war in Europe was almost over and everyone knew it. Germany was on the brink of being crushed between two powerful foes that were closing in on both sides of her country. From the east the mighty Russian Army rolled steadily toward Germany, and from the west a huge tank force led by the American General Patton was poised to strike at Germany's industrial heartland.

5

The Allied High Command was confident of a quick victory. Earlier in the year General Eisenhower had bet British General Montgomery five pounds (then twenty-five dollars) that the European war would be over by Christmas, 1944. In the middle of December, Eisenhower wrote Montgomery that he had yet to pay his bet because, "I still have nine days left."

But behind the lines at the Ardennes Forest thousands of German soldiers, supported by tanks and guns, were moving into attack position. These German troop movements were held in such secrecy that not even front-line soldiers were aware of the activity going on

behind them. Tanks were camouflaged during the day and moved only at night so that patroling Allied planes could not see them. Even when the huge tanks moved at night, straw was placed on the roads to muffle the noise of their clanking treads.

The German offensive that was about to break out had been planned almost entirely by one man—Adolf Hitler. At a staff meeting in September, a German general mentioned the Ardennes Forest.

"Stop!" Hitler commanded. Then he rose slowly from his chair. "That is where we will win this war. In the Ardennes."

For Hitler there was magic in the words "the Ardennes." For almost one hundred years the lush pine forests had been used by attacking German armies as an avenue to France. In 1940, Hitler's own tank forces had electrified the world by racing through the Ardennes and sweeping into France. At that time the German Army had introduced a new concept of warfare—*blitzkrieg*, lightning war. Tanks protected by airplanes rolled over French positions. The tanks were followed by infantrymen riding in trucks. The world had never seen an army move with such astonishing speed, and the Germans won victory after victory.

"History will repeat itself," Hitler told his generals. "We will launch an attack that no one can stop."

The Nazi leader hoped that one bold thrust would break the backs of the American, British, and French forces. Hitler believed the alliance between the Western Allies and the Russians was shaky and that if the West suffered a major defeat they would switch sides and join Germany in her fight against the Russians.

Hitler's thinking was that of a desperate man. The Western Allies and the Russians had enormous disagreements, but they were united in their effort to smash Nazi Germany. Many German generals told their *Führer* (leader) that it would not be possible to crack the alliance between the Russians and the West, but Hitler ignored them. He trusted no one. A few months earlier, in July, members of his own staff had tried to kill him by placing a bomb under a table near where he stood. The bomb exploded, but did not kill Hitler. Now, suspicious and alone, he prepared to launch what would be Germany's last offensive.

Secrecy was vital in planning this attack, for Hitler knew he must achieve complete surprise to succeed. IIe permitted only a few high-ranking generals to assist him with the preparation. Crack tank divisions were pulled out of Italy and the Russian front and moved into position behind the Ardennes. The newest and best tanks built in German factories were saved for this one attack. By December 15, Hitler had a quarter of a million men, almost two thousand heavy guns, and about one thousand tanks all poised to attack the unsuspecting units of the American Army in the Ardennes Forest.

On December 16, at five-thirty in the morning, German artillery officers issued a single command.

"Fire!"

The days of quiet along the Ardennes front were suddenly shattered by screaming shells and thundering explosions. Enormous 14-inch railway guns fired huge shells at special targets miles behind the American lines. Smaller shells barked out of the famous German 88-millimeter guns. Rockets sailed from rocket launchers, making a sound so terrifying the American GIs had named them "screaming meemies."

The Americans, most of them sleeping in foxholes, were awakened by the deafening explosions. The peaceful pine forest had suddenly turned into a nightmare of exploding shells. One terrified American, crouching in his foxhole during the barrage, was still strangely fascinated by what the artillery did to the forest scene. A moment before, the forest had looked

like a picture on a Christmas card; the pine trees had been elegantly decorated with light snow, and a blanket of snow covered the ground. Now snow had shaken from the shuddering trees and what once had been a dazzling white forest floor was scarred with shell holes and mud.

The artillery barrage lasted about an hour. Then a few minutes of silence settled on the front. It was a tense silence, in some ways more frightening than the din of constant explosions. Faintly, through the early morning fog, American soldiers heard the deep rumble of diesel engines and the unmistakable clanging of tank treads.

"Tanks," a GI called. "Tanks," another repeated. The word was passed from one group of
GIs to another. "German tanks coming up."

Bazooka teams crawled through the snow into
positions near the road. Anti-tank gunners
readied their weapons. The Americans peered
through the fog, waiting. Finally, out of the
mist, the lead German tank appeared, rolling
steadily over the forest road. Flanking the tank
were groups of German soldiers wearing white
snow uniforms. Crouching, they half walked and
half ran to keep up with the tank. To some of
the GIs the German soldiers moving through the
mist looked strangely like ghosts.

One American infantry officer, lying on his belly in the snow, peered at the leading German tank through binoculars. He was confused. He had never seen a tank like that before. Suddenly he realized what it was. "Oh no," he said to a sergeant lying next to him, "that's a Tiger."

Most American units in the Ardennes had never faced the new German Tiger tank. This dreaded tank weighed sixty tons, almost twice the weight of the American-built Sherman, and it mounted the powerful 88-millimeter gun.

As the lead Tiger tank rolled closer, the American crew of a 57-millimeter anti-tank gun took aim. Their gun cracked and spat out a shell. There was a sharp scraping sound and sparks flew from the Tiger. The huge tank stopped dead in its tracks. Then the tank's turret, like the head of a prehistoric monster, began to turn slowly, searching for the pest that had annoyed it. The American gun had scored a direct hit on the German tank, but the shell had bounced harmlessly off its thick armor.

Behind the lead German tank thousands of infantrymen were jammed into trucks. Hitler hoped his tank would roll over American front-line defenders and allow the infantry to penetrate deep into American lines. Most of the German soldiers were regular infantry, but there was also one small, carefully picked unit with a special mission.

Weeks before the offensive, Hitler summoned to his headquarters a colonel named Otto Skorzeny. Skorzeny was the most daring and skilled commando officer in the German Army.

"I have for you the most important job of your life," Hitler told Skorzeny. He explained how he wanted to gather a small group of Germans who spoke English and could fight behind the lines posing as Americans. Skorzeny was to train and command this unit. Wearing American uniforms and driving captured American vehicles they would destroy equipment, blow up supplies, and spread terror in rear-line American areas. Skorzeny smiled and accepted the assignment. It was precisely the kind of job he most enjoyed.

But Skorzeny's men could not be deployed until the Germans penetrated the American front, and the GIs were proving to be a stubborn foe.

After the start of the offensive, American lines wavered but held. Where front-line troops were overwhelmed, rear-echelon soldiers were ordered to fight. Cooks, bakers, and truck mechanics were given rifles and sent to the front.

One German tank commander lost two of his newest tanks to an American heavy anti-tank gun. He finally surrounded the gun and captured its crew. The German officer was amazed to discover that most of the crew were members of the division marching band who had set aside their horns and drums to join the fight. They had never before fired an anti-tank gun.

But there is an old saying among generals from all nations that a line cannot be strong everywhere. The Germans soon found an area in the Ardennes, a gap between two divisions, where there were practically no American defenders. German tanks and infantry poured through this gap and drove behind American lines. The American units that had held so bravely during the morning of the offensive were forced to retreat or face the danger of being surrounded. Also racing through this gap and into American territory were a handful of Skorzeny's English-speaking German soldiers wearing American uniforms and driving American jeeps.

The opening days of the offensive belonged to the Germans as their army advanced on all fronts. Even the weather seemed to favor the Germans. The thick fog that had gathered on the morning of the offensive remained and kept American airplanes on the ground. In Allied headquarters, on a huge map showing the positions of the battle lines, an ominous black bulge appeared in the north of Europe. History would remember that map, and the German offensive in the Ardennes would be forever called "the Battle of the Bulge."

Often this battle moved so fast that maps showing positions of opposing forces became meaningless. Confusion was a feeling shared by all soldiers during the Battle of the Bulge. At night one American tank was standing still on a forest roadside when it was suddenly bumped from behind by another tank. The American driver swore and yelled at the other tank to watch where he was going. The driver of the other tank said something that sounded like an apology, but his reply was in German. Then both tanks rumbled away from each other and into the night.

A few days after the German attack, an American tank officer who commanded five tanks wondered if he should destroy his tanks and surrender to the Germans. He was surrounded. The only road back to the American lines led through the town of St. Vith, and St. Vith had been captured by the Germans the previous night.

He decided not to surrender and instead ordered his tanks to try to dash through the little town. Pink flames and dark smoke poured from the houses of St. Vith as the five tanks approached. At the outskirts of the town the officer ordered his driver, "Give it everything you've got!"

With a great roar the tanks rolled single file into the flaming town and raced down the main street. Bullets from German rifles and machine guns bounced off the armor plates of the tank. The lead tank rounded a bend in the street and skidded to a stop. A burning American tank blocked the road.

"Which way should I go, left or right?" the desperate driver asked.

There seemed to be no way around the tank, and the commander was ready to say he didn't care which way the driver went, but he ordered, "Go right."

Before the tanks could start up again dozens of soldiers suddenly rushed toward them. Just as the tank commander was about to fire at them he realized the men were Americans. He reasoned they had somehow been left behind when their units evacuated the village, and had been hiding in the basements hoping to find a

way out. The men climbed on top of the tanks, and the dash through St. Vith continued.

The lead tank jerked right, scraped against a building, but managed to pull around the burning American tank. All five tanks, with scores of men clinging to them, squeezed past the destroyed tank and raced out of the town.

After he was a safe distance away from St. Vith, the tank commander opened the hatch on his turret and looked out. For the first time he noticed that two of the men riding on his tank were Germans. They were unarmed, probably prisoners of the Americans who had been trapped in the town.

As the commander's tank climbed over the snowy roads the men on board felt an overpowering sense of relief. Moments before, each one had been certain he was a dead man. Now their chances of surviving this battle had increased considerably. Though their situation was serious, it no longer seemed to be hopeless. They might even live to see Christmas. One GI on the lead tank began to sing.

"Silent night, holy night."

Before he was finished, everyone riding in the speeding tank had joined him. They sang the first verse over again, and this time the commander heard the voices of the two Germans.

"Stille Nacht, heilige Nacht."

At Allied headquarters General Eisenhower moved swiftly to stop the German advance. The men of two crack divisions, the 82nd and 101st Airborne Divisions, who had been resting in France, were rushed on trucks to the front. The 82nd was ordered to the town of Werbomont in Belgium, and the 101st raced to the town whose name would symbolize American resistance during the Battle of the Bulge—Bastogne.

To the south of the battle the huge U.S. Third Army was ordered to make a 90 degree turn and attack the German left flank. The Third Army was commanded by the fiery and forceful U.S. General George Patton. Patton promised Eisenhower that he would break the back of the German offensive in the Ardennes before Christmas. Every GI knew that Patton often drove his men and his tanks to the breaking point, but he got the job done.

A feeling of confidence grew among the Americans fighting in the Ardennes. "Patton's coming," they told each other. "Patton's on his way. He'll get us out of this mess."

Behind Allied lines, Colonel Skorzeny's men posing as Americans had done little damage. One of them, dressed as an American MP, had misdirected a column of U.S. trucks away from the front and onto a muddy road where the trucks bogged down, but the immense destruction Hitler expected from this unit never occurred. Too few of Skorzeny's special troops had managed to sneak through American lines to do any real damage.

Several days after the start of the battle two of Skorzeny's men, in an American jeep, noticed they were running out of gasoline. They decided to try to borrow some gas from some American trucks parked along the roadside.

The jeep slowed to a stop and the German driver, dressed in an American uniform, asked, "May we have some petrol, please?"

Obviously this German soldier had learned his English in England and the suspicious GIs seized the two men. More of Skorzeny's men were rounded up and the Americans soon discovered the German plan to place saboteurs behind their ranks.

Although Skorzeny's men did little damage while free, their capture was nearly a disaster for the Americans. Wild rumors spread from GI to GI that English-speaking Germans were everywhere, the original small number of German spies operating behind Allied lines became many hundreds in the minds of the American soldiers.

The rear areas became a nightmare of confusion. Americans were stopped and questioned for hours by other Americans who wondered which side they were really on. The questions asked were ones the GIs thought every American should know. Who is Mickey Mouse's girlfriend? Name the actors on the Amos and Andy radio show. Who are Donald Duck's three nephews?

Men on vital missions and others bearing important messages were delayed because they could not provide correct answers to what would

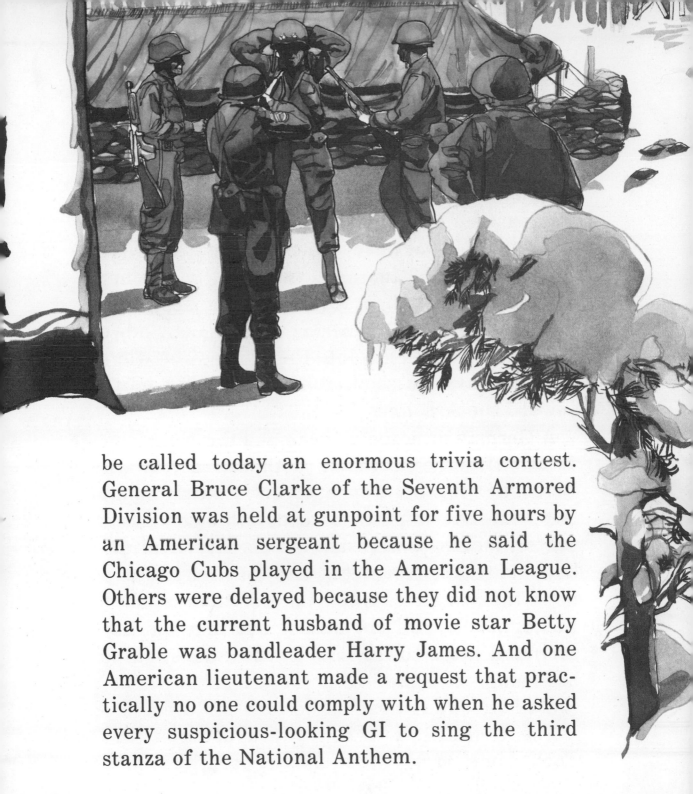

be called today an enormous trivia contest. General Bruce Clarke of the Seventh Armored Division was held at gunpoint for five hours by an American sergeant because he said the Chicago Cubs played in the American League. Others were delayed because they did not know that the current husband of movie star Betty Grable was bandleader Harry James. And one American lieutenant made a request that practically no one could comply with when he asked every suspicious-looking GI to sing the third stanza of the National Anthem.

Despite this confusion in the rear areas, American resistance stiffened, and the German advance slowed down. And from the south came Patton. The hard-driving general seemed to be everywhere all at once. Sometimes he joked with his men, other times he swore at them, but always he urged them forward as his jeep raced beside columns of lumbering tanks. "Let's move it, you men. Let's get into the action. The war's up this way," he shouted while pointing north toward the Ardennes.

A German armored division and the American 101st Airborne Division both raced toward Bastogne. Bastogne is a dreary-looking small city, but five important roads all meet in its center, making possession of this city vital for both sides. The Americans arrived first and dug in at the outskirts. When the Germans reached Bastogne they did not attack, but they quickly surrounded the town. Now it was a question of how long the Americans, cut off at Bastogne, could hold out against the relentless Germans.

The Germans launched attack after attack. Each time they were driven back, but the

American units in Bastogne were running out of ammunition. Their anti-tank guns were down to only five rounds each. Fresh supplies could be dropped by parachute, but the thick fog that settled throughout the Ardennes still favored the Germans. American supply planes would not be able to find the defenders of Bastogne through that fog.

On the morning of December 22, four German officers wearing overcoats that looked fresh from the cleaners approached an American sergeant billeted in a farmhouse just outside Bastogne. The Germans carried a white flag. The sergeant let them come close enough to talk and one of them said in very careful English, "We are German officers. We want to speak to your officers."

They were taken to the headquarters of General McAuliffe of the 101st Airborne Division. There the four Germans demanded an immediate surrender. They told the American general his troops were surrounded by powerful forces, and his position was hopeless.

Impatiently, McAuliffe listened to the German officers. He had work to do, and thought this talk was a waste of time. When the Germans were finished talking, he stood, put his hands on his hips, and said, "Aw, nuts." With that he told the Germans to return to their own lines. The Germans were confused by McAuliffe's reply and asked for a written answer.

"All right," McAuliffe said. "You want it in writing, I'll give it to you in writing."

He sat down and typed out what has become one of the most famous answers to a demand for surrender in all history:

> To: The German Commander.
>   NUTS!
> From: The American Commander.

On December 23 the Americans surrounded at Bastogne received an early Christmas present. The dense fog that had been aiding the Germans since the start of the offensive faded. At noon a flight of C-47 cargo planes roared over the town, discharging tons of supplies. The supplies float-

ed to earth on brightly colored parachutes looking like swarms of summertime butterflies. GIs
and Belgian civilians danced in the streets at
the sight.

On the day after Christmas a tank battalion
under the command of Colonel Creighton
Abrams, who was later to command the U.S.
Army in Vietnam, broke through the German
defenders and roared into Bastogne. Abrams'
unit was the spearhead of George Patton's Third
Army. Led by the relentless Patton, the Third
Army had crashed into the German left flank
and raced toward Bastogne. But the Battle of
the Bulge had proved that General Patton was
only human after all. He had promised Eisenhower he would be in Bastogne by Christmas,
and he was one day late.

With Patton's army in Bastogne the tide of war was reversed. Now many German units, to avoid being surrounded, were forced into frenzied retreat.

Weeks of fighting remained, but the great German retreat was on. After Christmas the weather turned so bitterly cold that frostbite produced more casualties than bullets. The American advance was slowed by the cold weather, but that great black bulge that once loomed on the map of northern Europe steadily receded and the American lines advanced toward the Rhine River and into Germany.

The German offensive in the Ardennes that became famous as the Battle of the Bulge was a desperate attempt to reverse the course of the war. The offensive had been initiated by a desperate man—Adolf Hitler. At the start of

World War II Hitler promised the German people an empire that would last one thousand years. His early victories had convinced him that the German Army was superior to all others and that he was a military genius. But as the war drew to a close, Germany's once mighty army was retreating on all fronts, and Germany itself was a shambles.

On May 7, 1945, less than four months after the start of the attack at Ardennes, Germany surrendered to the Allies. Adolf Hitler, once the most feared and powerful figure in Europe, was dead. He had committed suicide.

Lush pines stand in the Ardennes today, and the forest still looks its prettiest during the winter. It is difficult to imagine that one of the most massive battles in history was fought in these peaceful woods. But even today visitors can find the remains of the foxholes that American soldiers once called home. Perhaps these decaying foxholes can be thought of as true monuments to the courage of the American infantrymen who fought the Battle of the Bulge.

DATE D